DESTINATION
Italy

A Life's Journey with Divine Guidance

MILLY BORN

WESTBOW·
PRESS
A DIVISION OF THOMAS NELSON
& ZONDERVAN

Cover photo by Milly Born: "Mist Rising"

I have blotted out your transgressions like a cloud
and your sins like mist;
return to me, for I have redeemed you.
(Isaiah 44:22)

WestBow Press books may be ordered through booksellers or by contacting:

WestBow Press
A Division of Thomas Nelson & Zondervan
1663 Liberty Drive
Bloomington, IN 47403
www.westbowpress.com
1 (866) 928-1240

ISBN: 978-1-4908-3058-2 (sc)
ISBN: 978-1-4908-3059-9 (e)

Library of Congress Control Number: 2014905051

Printed in the United States of America.

WestBow Press rev. date: 05/27/2014

To you who seek to find your life.

To you who found and share the way.

To You who loves and seeks us all
To bring us close to You.
You reached out, showed me the way
To truth and life anew.

Contents

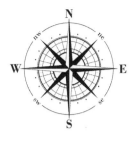

Foreword

I have the huge privilege of writing a foreword to this inspiring book about the Born family's courageous journey into the center of God's will. Milly's narrative invites us to journey with them into a discovery of a deeper and more meaningful relationship with God, the pains and emotions of childlessness and the realization of the high call to plant a church. We share in their triumphs in buying a house, in becoming parents, and in pioneering a church plant. In the process, we are introduced to the rich and unique Italian culture!

Adele (my wife) and I met Jan and Milly some time back, and what struck us immediately was their big hearts and passion for Jesus. They travelled all the way from Orvieto to San Romano and back (a 2-hour journey one-way) to sit with us for an hour! We knew that, in this short time, God had knitted our hearts together, and so began an important relationship for us.

Adele and I pastor a church in Johannesburg, South Africa, that works in partnership with New Covenant Ministries International (NCMI). Part of NCMI's apostolic call is to trust God for churches to be planted in every country, city, and village. We made contact with Jan and Milly through their enrolment in our correspondence study program. We were excited at the opportunity to help support a church plant in the "heart" of Italy. Through this initial contact, and the other churches we work with both in Italy and South Africa, Jan and Milly's house has become the place where many of us have visited. Every visitor remarks on the peace and tranquility of the place, and the times of refreshing they experienced there—warm hospitality and peacefulness.

It is a joy to partner with them in seeing people born again in their region and integrated into the local church they have planted. Little by little, they are preparing for a promised harvest. They are focused also on supporting any church God links them with and have a dedicated intercessory prayer focus on revival in Italy. Their passion is infectious!

However, the most emotionally stirring event we have walked through with them has been seeing them become parents. We will leave that detail out and let you read it for yourselves. Those chapters are filled with hope and joy.

This short look into their lives will engross you, fascinate you, bring you to tears and encourage you to trust God as they have, because God is faithful! We look forward to their continued journey and the many more lives they will certainly impact for the Kingdom of God.

Marcus and Adele Herbert
Cornerstone Church
Johannesburg, South Africa

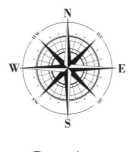

Preface

About eight years ago, someone told me that I would write, and that God would use my words to touch many people's hearts. Since then, I have asked God to reveal to me what I should write to step into that prophesy. It is true that I have always loved to write but, previously, I have written only promotional texts, blog posts, and short meditations, along with many books full of technical information that I produced during my professional career. What did God want me to write now? Bible studies? A novel perhaps? However, I am not a fiction writer; I simply don't have the imagination. I remember how intrigued I was as a kid as I watched my younger brother playing with his model cars, making up wonderful stories as he pushed the toys across the carpet's pattern, which served as the roads of the village where the imaginary owners of the cars lived. Maybe the lack of imagination made me a good technical writer, but it has also made me wonder where to find the words that touch hearts.

Then one day my husband Jan and I talked about a book he was reading. It was written by an American lady, and it contained beautiful short stories about her own and other people's experiences with God.

"Do you realize that we too could fill a book about what God has done in our lives? How he guided us and still does to bring us to our destiny?" Jan said.

We talked a while about the moments we felt his hand leading us, sometimes gently, other times with a strong nudge, and about the occasions in which we recognize his guidance only with hindsight. Where we are now, what we are doing, and what we will do; it is all because he wanted us to be right here and to do exactly this, from the beginning of our lives. It is the very purpose of our existence.

Slowly but surely, the idea to write a book about God's guidance was conceived in my mind. Could I? This wasn't fantasy but real-life stuff, so I probably could. Okay, but then, should I? Was that what God wanted me to do? Would those touching words be in there? When I spoke of my thoughts, Jan's reaction was positive. In fact, we were both excited and began brainstorming about the structure and content of that possible book. A few days and many prayers later, we were sure that it was God's will. Therefore, not only is the content of this book about divine guidance, but the book itself is a result of it.

God's purposes in day-to-day events and experiences are not always easy to discern. By sharing our story, I hope to encourage you to reflect and recognize God's guidance in your own life, so that you too may reach your purpose and divine destiny. I pray that you may feel his love and experience the thrill while you discover the path. May God bless you with his peaceful presence, wherever he will lead you.

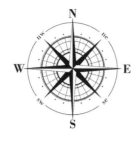

Acknowledgments

Thank you, my loving husband Jan, who shared the most important part of my journey. You went ahead of me, because you believed in God's purposes for my life. Your unfailing faith will always be an example to me. I love you.

Thank you, my lovely daughter, my little traveling companion. You are the most wonderful gift of God during my life's adventure. I love you and cherish the special bond between us.

Thank you, my friends and first readers Joan Marran, Lindsay Jenks, and Celeste Allan. Your enthusiastic feedback encouraged me to publish this story. Your comments helped me to fill in some gaps and increase the readability. Your prayers will forever boost our journey.

Thank you, my friend and first-class editor Sara Taylor. We have traveled together in the past and shared fun—and some heartaches—along the way. I highly value your friendship. Your final touch lifted this book to a higher level. (The only reason for any grammar and spelling mistakes is that I have rewritten quite a few paragraphs *after* your edit!)

Thank you, Marcus and Adele Herbert. You are a wonderful couple—an example to us—and your apostolic-prophetic support always encourages us to move forward to our spiritual destination, here in the heart of Italy.

Thank you, Jesus. You are my Guide, my Goal, my God.

CHAPTER ONE

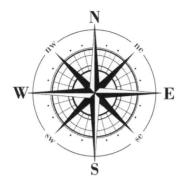

The Call

France, March 2004

The sky was grey. Trees and bushes were still bare after another long winter, and a hard wind tugged at the branches. The old farmhouse was chilly. I pulled my cardigan closer around my body as I went outside to get some more wood. When I came back in the kitchen with a basket full of logs, the telephone rang. I put the basket on the black and white checkered floor and picked up the phone from the heavy wooden table.

"Domaine du Vieux Chêne, bonjour!"

"Hey, it's me! I am just calling to let you know I'm headed in the right direction!" I heard Jan say, almost shouting with joy. "I spotted flowers along the road! Spring has already begun here!"

His words warmed me at least as much as the stove did. We were ready to live in a milder climate after having lived more than five years in the Haut-Languedoc at an altitude of around 3,000 feet and enduring long, cold winters. Jan was on his way to Italy to prepare for a new start to our life. Yet again.

The first time had been in December 1998, when we moved from the Netherlands to France to live out the dream of many Dutch people—running a campsite in the south of France. Jan was forty-seven years and I thirty-seven. We had given up our business careers, bought an old farmhouse with some land around it, built the campsite, and made it a success. That is the story in a tiny nutshell.

During the first years, I had panicked every time Jan talked about the possibility of moving on, changing life one more time and leaving our *domaine*, which was set on a hillside among woods and within close proximity to a beautiful lake. Each time we had waved goodbye to the guests who, after their holiday, went back home, I had felt relieved; I didn't have to go away. I didn't want to leave that gorgeous spot, not for all the gold in the world, in spite of the long winters which, of course, we hadn't foreseen when we actually moved there. In fact, one week after our arrival, we found ourselves caught in a blizzard on the parking lot of a supermarket, trying to get the groceries into the back of our Land Rover. The next day we woke up in a white world, with snow at least 1.5 feet deep! However, Jan had always known that France was a temporary station for us. He just felt it, and while his faith and his relationship with God deepened in the isolation of the

French countryside, he grew more certain about it. I had arrived in France without any faith, any god.

I was born into a non-believing family. Officially, my mother was Protestant and my father Catholic. They were both baptized as babies, but neither of them believed. My father was very explicit about this matter. As a boy growing up in Amsterdam, he had lived through the atrocities of the Second World War. He saw how Jewish people were rounded up, how innocent people were shot to death, how his own father died of starvation and his body decomposed because no one took care of it. In fact, he had hardly survived himself during that last war winter before the allies set the country free. Immediately after the liberation, just twelve years old, he was placed in a Christian farming family in the countryside to regain his strength, but there he received only the leftovers from their well-stocked table, and little warmth to nourish his soul. Later, while studying at a Roman Catholic school, he witnessed how the Catholic Brothers who taught at the school were unable to keep their hands to themselves. As an adult, he also experienced much disillusionment. He had to work with lying and stealing people, including many so-called Christians, while he always followed his feelings of what was right and fair.

In our family, we believed that God didn't exist, couldn't exist. First, because we couldn't imagine that he would allow so much injustice in the world. In addition, if Christianity was what the many professed believers were practicing, it was worth nothing. Finally, because it simply wasn't intelligent to believe in something that you could not see. Plainly said, we thought that Christians were no-brain hypocrites.

From the time he was in his forties, Dad was severely stressed and never worked again. He was a disappointed man, a psychologically broken man. However, although he had little formal education, he was also a very smart man—one of the most broadly developed people I have ever met in my life. To him, intelligence was the highest good. He encouraged my brother, sister, and me to study and to get important jobs and, thereby, to earn other people's respect. It would also help us to remain in command over our own lives, so that we would never become victims of injustice ourselves, or so he thought. He wanted us to be tough, to put ourselves first, and to speak up, because "modest people turn out shitty." He wanted nothing but good for us, to prevent us from having to go through the same heartbreak that he had experienced.

At the end, my father was ill, very ill. In addition to the damage caused by several heart attacks, a cruel disease had gradually diminished his lung capacity. The lack of oxygen ruined his organs, and he was in constant pain. Nurses who visited my parents' house several times a day to help care for my father said that they had never seen a person so ill. He was afraid to die and held on to life as long as possible on pure will power.

Then one day, when he was extremely short of breath and suffered tremendously, the family doctor suggested morphine. Not for the first time, but until that moment Dad had refused the drug, because he didn't want to lose control. This time he agreed. The medicine removed not only his pain, but also his consciousness and, finally, his volition to keep breathing. He died at the age of sixty-nine, within half an hour after the first drips seeped into his devastated body. He didn't outlive my mother, who was ten years older.

I was not there. Oh, I had been in the Netherlands, but work had called me back to France. It was May, and we had to finish building the last cottage and prepare the campsite for the arrival of the first guests by the end of that month. Moreover, I had assured myself that I would come back to see Dad on his birthday, just one week later. I had even asked the doctor if there was any risk of my father dying during my absence. He had answered that he didn't see any medical reason for it. Therefore, I left, and Dad died, two days before his seventieth birthday, while I was working nine hundred miles away. My brother and sister told me that his last words were, "I hope Milly won't be angry with me." He had known that the morphine would do more than relieve the tightness in his chest.

Losing my father was extremely painful, and the fact that I hadn't been there when he died made the loss even more difficult. It was as if someone had closed the book of his life before I could read the last chapter. I needed time to mourn, but when we came back from the Netherlands after the cremation, I just didn't have the time. Tourist season had begun. Anyone who has ever run a campsite, a hotel, or any other tourist accommodation knows that, during the season, you live for your guests. There is no time for you. Although we had always loved meeting new people and contributing to their holidays, that summer I found it difficult to find pleasure in their company or the work. In addition, it turned out to be a particularly hot summer. Sometimes the temperature in the kitchen was over 100 degrees as I cooked yet another evening meal for thirty people. My heart was heavy, and my body was tired. Every now and then, I managed to cry in the car on my way to the supermarket, but that wasn't enough to lift the burden of sadness.

In September, after we had waved goodbye to the last guests, I collapsed. Always before, we had simply stayed at home to recover after summer, enjoying the silence and the wonder of nature in the short, golden autumn before winter would arrive again. That year, however, we felt the need to go on a real holiday, even if it would be only one week, and we opted for Italy. I had visited Umbria almost ten years before with a dear friend from work, just two days, and cherished sweet memories of the green heart of Italy: rolling hills, vast woods, and cities covered with history's fingerprints. I wanted to go back there. Jan had always had a tender spot for Italy, so he willingly agreed.

As I browsed the Internet for possible destinations, I discovered several websites of real estate agencies that offered not only accommodation for rent but also for sale. Jan caught me one afternoon while I was dreaming away with pictures of farms on hills and olive groves under the Umbrian sun, and I said to him, half-joking, "What about selling the campsite, buying a farm in Umbria and growing olives?"

He took his gaze off the computer screen, locked his eyes with mine, and answered, wholly serious, "Yes, that's it! Let's do it."

To Jan, it was clear that God had spoken to us, while I simply felt an inexplicable longing. We had no clue why we had to go to the heart of Italy but, at the same time, we were confident that everything would be all right. Although we were both ready to sell the campsite and move instantly, we tried to keep our heads cool and act as the former business people we were. Who in their right mind would emigrate without even trying to get the look and feel of their future home? And, after all, we needed that holiday. Therefore, I booked a week in a lovely villa in Umbria, owned by an English couple who ran a bed and breakfast and, in addition, owned a thriving real estate business. It was the perfect combination for our "orientation mission," as we had called our holiday. The main purpose was to get an idea about whether we liked the region. Second, we wanted to find out about the costs of houses, the practicalities of immigration, and the possibilities for making a living. After that week we wanted to be able to say, based on both feelings and facts, "yes, we go," or "no, we won't go."

While we cleaned and put things in order on the campsite after the summer season, we often spoke about having an olive grove. We even visited one in the Hérault region of France to learn about the technical and economical aspects of growing olives. An important conclusion was that we wouldn't be able to live all year long off the yield of an olive grove the size we could handle. In other words, we would need to develop another activity, along with the olive oil production. We made long calculations and explored many real estate websites.

Finally, in the first week of November, we left our mini-zoo (cats, dogs, goats, horses, ponies, donkey, and chicken) in the caring hands of a good friend who came over from the Netherlands and we headed for Italy. We flew to Rome and rented a small car at the airport. In our suitcase, we brought a file containing all the information we had gathered, including a list of properties that might be interesting. In our hearts, we carried a fire that wouldn't be smothered.

CHAPTER TWO

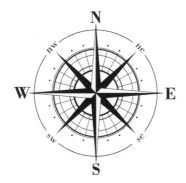

The Confirmation

Italy, November 2004

*E*arly sunlight, filtering through white curtains, woke me up that first morning in Umbria. My mind slowly became accustomed to the unfamiliar but tasteful environment. I was lying in a wrought-iron double bed under a white-painted, beamed ceiling. The bed had beautifully embroidered sheets. Next to me, Jan was still asleep. I got dressed as quietly as possible and sneaked out of the room, down the stairs and outside, where I found a few Italian builders working on the natural stone wall of an annex next to the villa. The air was still cool, but I could already feel the warmth of the sun on my face. I wondered what time it was. In my best Italian, which came directly from an Italian phrase book for beginners, I asked the builders and was surprised to find out that it was an hour earlier than I supposed.

After I had pondered this for a while, I realized that this place was much further east than where we lived, so it saw the sun rise earlier. Pleased that I had resolved the mystery, I looked around and took in the surroundings. The autumn sun gave a golden touch to houses, vineyards, and trees, which were still covered with green leaves. I took a deep breath of Umbrian air, mixed with the smell of fresh mortar, and was filled with a great sense of anticipation.

Later, at the breakfast table on the roof terrace, enchanted by the wonderful view on the Tiber valley, which gradually became clearer as the morning haze dissolved, Jan and I looked at each other over our first cup of cappuccino and just knew that one day Umbria would be our home. Nevertheless, before we allowed ourselves to say that aloud, we had a to-do list to complete. First action point: get an idea of the value for money on the housing market.

Before long, we were on our way to the first property, at the north of Perugia. We had found it on the organization's website and had fallen in love with the pictures of the huge olive trees that were at least a hundred years old. Dora, the real estate agent, drove us there in her car. As we approached the property, the roadway that took us uphill narrowed, and then the pavement vanished. Dora explained that the Italian countryside still has many dirt roads, simply because the communities don't have the money to pay for asphalt. Upon arrival, the olive grove exceeded our expectations, with its well-maintained rows of lush trees loaded with olives, ready to pick. The trees were pruned in the typical open-vase shape, with three or four main stems coming from the single lower trunk and open in the center to allow light in. Furthermore, the view from the property was stunning. It was as if we could see all of Umbria, with Perugia glistening in the valley below.

Unfortunately, the house was horrible. It was a simple rectangular building, once an authentic Umbrian farmhouse, but now spoiled by someone who had tried to "modernize" it. Judging by the color scheme, the lathed walls, and the ugly floor tiles, the modernization had taken place in the seventies. To make things worse, all internal walls had been removed, leaving a big open space that would be difficult to heat. Outside, a modern portico marred one of the natural stone walls. Sure, it would be possible to restore the house to its original condition, but the costs on top of the rather high purchase price would be far beyond our budget.

To Jan, the whole thing was a "no-go," but I found it difficult to say goodbye to the olive trees and the view. That was why we returned at the end of that day, after having seen two other villas with even less promise, just so that I could be sure it would be the right decision not to buy the very first place we had visited. Sitting on a low wall, we saw the sun set behind the Umbrian hills and the city lights of Perugia turn on. Quietly, we talked again about all the reasons why this property was not a good idea. Moreover, we had not come to buy at this moment; we first needed to sell the campsite in France.

When we finally rose to leave, Jan walked ahead of me in the cool evening air. I lingered and, in one long last look, tried to absorb the view in the now bluish light. After a deep sigh, I turned around and followed my husband to the car.

Before returning to our B&B, we parked our car just outside of Perugia and walked up stairs and through narrow, winding alleys into the historic center to get a taste of what might become "our" city. When we reached the *Corso Vannucci*, I felt that I had stepped into a movie set. Bathed in silvery light, a wide pedestrian avenue led between massive historic buildings to a huge cathedral. A large, three-layered, medieval fountain stood in front of it, water gushing from an amphora held up by three bronze nymphs in the upper basin. Could it really be true that one day we would live here?

I don't remember exactly how many properties we saw the first days of our holiday, but the conclusion was that if we were to buy a house in the green heart of Italy, we would not have the money to have it renovated; we would have to do it ourselves. This didn't deter us though, because in France we had learned how to build, plaster, and paint. We also worked on the additional action points in our to-do list. We quickly learned a lot about the Italian bureaucracy, for example, how to avoid catch-22 situations such as "before you can buy a house in Italy, you must have a bank account; before you can open a bank account, you must have a fiscal code; before you can get a fiscal code, you must be a resident in Italy."

Obviously, we didn't really relax while doing the property inspections and procedural research. Our minds were in constant motion, so we decided to take a break and explore the region as tourists. We planned an outing to the white city on the hillside of Mount Subasio, the city where Saint Francis was born and died: Assisi. After another tasty breakfast on the roof terrace, we drove across Umbria, thoroughly enjoying the landscape: woods, freshly plowed fields, hilltop cities, and a sun that never stopped shining. Italians call this period of beautiful weather *"l'estate di San Martino,"* Saint Martin's summer, referring to this saint's feast-day on November 11. All the while, we couldn't stop chatting about our plans to come and live here. Keeping his eyes on the road, Jan said, "Do you realize we have already decided?"

"Yes, we have, haven't we?" I answered, my voice shrill with excitement. When I looked at Jan's face, I saw he was beaming with the same joy that I felt in my heart. Suddenly he pulled the car over to the side of the road. Surprised, I asked, "Hey, what's wrong?"

He stopped the engine, turned towards me, and said, "There's nothing wrong. I just would like to pray to my Father, now that we're on the edge of a new beginning. I know that you don't believe as I do but, please, will you join me?"

I hesitated and pushed away the feelings of irritation. I didn't want to fake a faith that I didn't have. However, I did feel a fire, a fire for Umbria. I could feel it burning right then, right there. How was it possible that I wanted to leave our paradise in France? That I didn't shrink from the idea of leaving everything we had worked on so hard during the past five years and begin something completely new? When we had finished the construction of the last tourist accommodation only this year and we would finally have time to sit back and enjoy? Now that we finally had made real friends? Yet, something–or Someone?–somehow, had placed a longing inside of me that I couldn't ignore. Jan looked at me, waiting for an answer.

"Okay, pray," I said softly.

He took my hands in his, closed his eyes and prayed.

"Dear Father God, we come before you to thank you for your guidance. We feel the confirmation in our hearts that we really should move to this region. I know that you have a purpose in all of this, although I don't understand it yet. I simply trust you. Please keep leading us in every step we take, so that we can walk into the destiny that you have planned for us. In Jesus' name I pray, amen."

He let go of my hands and started the car again. We continued the journey to Assisi, less talkative, more thoughtful now. I felt a peace and certainty that seemed out of place, given our situation. Where did these feelings come from?

Assisi was impressive in many ways. Medieval architecture, narrow streets, and beautiful views over surrounding hills and valleys gave the city a timeless atmosphere, although the abundance of souvenir shops and busloads of pilgrims detracted from the picturesque scenery. Jan found it painful to see how various saints and the Virgin Mary were venerated and, besides, how this unbiblical devotion was being commercially exploited. To me, it was simply a weird mixture of religion and business. Wasn't faith supposed to be free of financial interest?

My confusion increased when we visited the Cathedral of Saint Francis. From the information I read beforehand, I had learned that Francis was completely dedicated to God and lived a humble life following Jesus' example, including detachment from material goods. One of his quotes was, "The brothers shall not acquire anything as their own, neither a house nor a place nor anything at all." He died in 1226 at the age of forty-five. Then, within two years after his death, the pope canonized him, and the people of Assisi started the construction of a huge, decorated cathedral to honor their hometown saint. They couldn't have acted in a way more contrary to his teachings, which focused on Jesus Christ, without a touch of self-importance.

From an artistic point of view, however, the *basilica,* with its three levels, was incredibly beautiful. Inside the church, we found ourselves in the midst of throngs of people–tourists from all over the world and many pilgrims who were, judging by their garments, from various Catholic orders. As we walked around, we admired the exultant, gothic heights of the upper *basilica,* which suggested that the church itself was reaching into heaven, an illusion that was reinforced by the dark blue ceiling, decorated with golden stars. Endless frescoes covered the walls and depicted, among other themes, scenes from the Bible and the life of Francis. The atmosphere became darker as we descended.

The lower church, built in Romanesque style, had a low ceiling with ribbed vaults, all frescoed, and many chapels dedicated to various saints where people were praying. Going down yet another stairway, we entered the crypt housing the tomb of Francis.

No frescoes here. A few, strategically placed lamps lit the space soberly. Our attention could go nowhere but to the stone shrine above the altar, especially because everyone was staring in that direction. We saw men, women, and children kissing the altar and praying to the remains of a person who died almost 800 years ago. I felt Jan become indignant as we queued up with the other visitors and walked around the tomb.

Once we stood outside again, our eyes squinting in the bright autumn sun, he almost choked on his words while he explained why he didn't understand. "We have a living God, yet people come here and pray to the bones of a dead man? Who has taught them to do that? How do they think God feels about this?"

Although I didn't share his feelings of indignation, I understood his reasoning. We had plenty to talk about in the car as we headed back.

That night Jan dreamed about walking between Jesus and Mary without experiencing negative feelings. Was Jan's Father trying to tell him that he should become accustomed to the idea of being around Catholic people without getting angry with them?

The day before our return to France, we went to see the last two properties on our list, both of them in Cerqueto, a small hamlet a stone's throw away from where we were staying. Before we visited the house, Gregory, the owner of the B&B and real estate agency, stopped at a small Catholic church and said, "This is why I love Umbria: it's one huge museum! Inside this simple church, you will find an early work of Pietro Vannucci, who was a famous 14th century painter. He lived and worked in Perugia; that is why they called him *Il Perugino*. The main street of Perugia, the *Corso Vannucci*, is named after him."

We stepped into the quiet of the empty church and saw a rather sober interior with white and beige walls and wooden pews. I caught a faint scent of incense as Gregory led us to one of the altars on the right and said, proudly, "Here it is."

The fresco was beautiful, although part of it had been lost when the original church was restored in the 18th century. The remaining large fragment depicted Saint Sebastian, tied to a pillar and pierced with arrows, in delicate colors, and of exceptional quality. The thought of studying art history crossed my mind. *A country so rich in cultural history will be a stimulating environment. Perhaps I can even market myself as a tour guide and organize inspiring art tours in Umbria?* When we left the church to continue our journey, I stored the idea in a corner of my brain to talk about with Jan later.

The first property we visited in Cerqueto was a narrow, three-story house in the village, with a view over the fields. Although it was cheap, it was not what we were looking for. The second property was merely a ruin on a slight slope in the midst of ploughed fields, with a beautiful view of the surrounding hills. It had once housed a farmer's family; now it gave shelter to a solitary tree that rose out of the roof. We would have to demolish and rebuild it completely. The fair price left enough on the budget for reconstruction, and we did love the spot. We considered buying a caravan and living there while we built our dream house. We had one problem, though; what to do with the horse and the pony that we planned to bring with us from France? The owner of the house was selling only two acres of ground around the house. We decided to let him know that we were seriously interested in buying, on condition that he sold us an extra four acres of land, so that we could make a meadow and add a shed for the animals. Gregory promised to contact the owner in our name and agreed that he would let us know as soon as possible.

That evening, during dinner in a lovely restaurant, I shared the idea of studying art history and combining my future knowledge with a touristic activity to supplement the income of the olive grove we yet had to acquire. Jan actually liked the idea, and we brainstormed about the possibilities. I could combine sports with art, offering bicycle tours through beautiful villages with hidden art treasures, such as the fresco in the small church of Cerqueto. Additionally, I could organize trips to small villages to visit local museums and to shop at the local markets. Later, a real Italian *mamma* could teach our guests how to prepare an authentic Italian meal with the freshest ingredients. We had much fun as ideas bubbled up and took shape while we discussed them. We even came up with the name of my new activity:

"Umbria from the Inside Out." It was a great last night before heading back home.

The next morning, the weather changed dramatically. Rain was pouring down, and a chill wind made the humidity even more uncomfortable. However, in the car on our way to the airport, we were glowing with enthusiasm. We had definitely decided to move to Umbria. We were even ready to make an offer to buy the Cerqueto ruin! What if it was possible to buy the extra land? The price was not high, but we still had to sell our campsite. Had we acted too swiftly? We talked about the option of the caravan although, honestly, this idea had become less attractive now that the climatic conditions had deteriorated. Then we had the idea of buying the village house in Cerqueto and living there while we worked on the other house. And, in case the owner of the ruin chose not to sell the four acres, we could still go and live there while searching for another property. Our excitement further increased with this new idea, and Jan even tried to reach Gregory, but could not contact him.

While we continued our journey to Rome, Jan calmed down and began to think about the many reasons why making a rash decision might not be a good idea. We decided not to contact the realtor, but to wait for the reaction to our proposal.

In the meantime, we traveled through dark woods over Mount Peglia, a mountain with an altitude of almost 3,000 feet, and the environment looked rather gloomy in the rain. At the top of the mountain, we drove past a group of hunters who had gathered on a parking place. The men were dressed in camouflage clothing and their rifles glistened in the damp air. The whole setting reminded us of the cold weather that we had left in France and of the French hunters with whom we had a difficult relationship. We once quarreled with one we had caught in the pasture in front of our house, as he ran between our horses while shooting at a deer. Another time we awoke, alarmed, suspecting that a war had begun outside our bedroom window. What we found instead was a neighbor, who had just shot a pheasant on our premises and, obviously, he hadn't hit the poor bird with the first shot.

While the wipers swished the water off our windshield, I shivered and said to Jan, "I don't want to live in this kind of area anymore, surrounded by woods, and I don't want to see any more hunters close to our new place."

Jan agreed wholeheartedly, and we talked about how the Perugia area seemed more open, more welcoming. Of one mind, we drove down the mountain towards Orvieto, where we would take the A1 highway to Rome.

Little did we know that our plans didn't match with the one Jan's Father had for us.

CHAPTER THREE

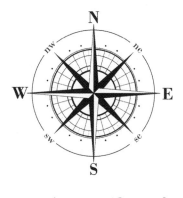

The Sale

*T*wo days after we came back home to France, Gregory called to give us the news that the owner of the ruin in Cerqueto didn't want to sell more land. By then, we didn't mind. It had been fun to dream, but somehow we felt that something else, more suitable, would come up.

Meanwhile, we had already created a small website as an online ad for our campsite and made sure it would be easy to find through the search engines. I had also ordered an Italian computer course and some Italian dictionaries, and begun to learn the language. Jan began to write an instruction guide for the new owners of our *domaine*. After we had put ads in some newspapers to point potential buyers to the website, we received several serious inquiries. We talked with people on the phone and sent emails with additional information but, before Christmas, no one had actually come to inspect our property.

We had not spoken to anyone in France about our plans to move away, because we didn't know how long it would take to sell; we didn't want to upset friends and customers before anything was certain. Our family and friends in the Netherlands, however, did know about our plans. My brother and sister, in particular, had to know, because they had proposed that we scatter my father's ashes under an impressive ancient oak tree–*le vieux chêne*–on our land. The first year we lived in France, we created a terrace under that tree, from which you could look over the valley with its spacious pasture for our horses and woods on both sides, leading down to a sparkling lake. My parents had visited us several times, and my father, a nature worshiper at heart, had fallen in love with the oak and the view. It would be the perfect spot for his remains, but it felt awkward to leave him there while we took off for Italy. My brother and sister insisted nonetheless, so they planned to come over for Christmas–probably our last in France–and bring my mother as well.

Having my family around–my mother, my brother's family, and my sister with her husband–made Christmas special that year. I noticed, though, that my mother was getting increasingly forgetful, and remembered that my father had already worried about that problem. She also looked tired and had problems walking at a normal pace. I dismissed my fears; after all, she was eighty years old.

We talked a lot about my father, not only with a sense of melancholy but also with joy. We laughed together as we remembered his silly jokes. He had been a very intelligent man, but while we were still children, he had often embarrassed us with his unconventional sense of humor. We deferred the moment of scattering his ashes as long as possible, perhaps because this final act would confirm his death definitively and irrevocably.

Finally, on an especially cold day, we gathered under the oak, next to the terrace. I shivered in the wintry breeze, in spite of the sunrays that peeked through the tree's enormous branches and covered us all with bright spots. A feeling of uneasiness settled upon us as we stood there with serious faces. One by one, my brother, my sister, and I took the urn and gradually scattered its contents.

When it was my turn, the wind slightly intensified, just long enough to take hold of the powdery substance before it touched the leaf-covered soil, and almost, almost blew it in my face. In spite of the solemn moment, I couldn't help but think of the famous scene in the movie *The Big Lebowski* and had to suppress an almost uncontrollable urge to laugh out loud. It was Dad's final joke.

That Christmas helped me to close the book of my father's life. I was ready for a brand-new story.

On a rainy day in January 2004, a young Dutch couple came to visit us. In the company of the woman's father, they were touring in the south of France, looking for a campsite that the father could buy and the couple would run. For some reason, we didn't click. Together we walked around our beloved *domaine* where we had worked hard for five years, spending blood, sweat, and tears to make it our dream place, and we heard them talking about all the ideas they had to change this, demolish that, improve here, and build there… in other words, they wanted to modify the whole atmosphere! Their plan was to transform our small, quiet, rustic hideaway into a big, commercial venture. We tried to swallow the frustration. After all, we were the ones who wanted to leave and sell our dream; we couldn't blame them for wanting to pursue their own. They left with a promise to contact us again.

A few days later, with rain still engulfing us, another couple came, representing a group of retired friends who were looking for a residence where they could spend the rest of their lives. Unlike the other couple, they wanted to stop all tourist activity and barter away the goodwill that we had built. More swallowing of disappointment on our side.

The third couple, Tim and Mara, came one week later. The rain had turned to snow, but a friendly sun had melted away most of it. After some mental preparation to brace ourselves for more violations, we showed them around the house and the fields. They loved every brick we had laid and every tree we had planted. Almost relieved, we invited them for lunch the next day to give them another opportunity to get to know the property.

I had set a table outside, in the welcoming warmth of the winter sun, so that the remnants of snowdrifts around the house wouldn't discourage them. During lunch, they told us a bit about their lives. Together with two brothers, Tim was co-owner of a garage. Mara had worked for an employer but left because of a conflict, and shared that it had been a painful experience. They had two children, five and three years old. When Mara refused the glass of wine we offered, she told us that she was one month pregnant with their third baby.

"Wow, congratulations!" Jan and I exclaimed. I was quick to calculate that she would be due in August, in the middle of the tourist season.

"So if you decided to buy the campsite, you would come in autumn," I assumed, disheartened. Now that we had found potential buyers we liked, would we need to work another summer? I dreaded the idea.

"Oh no," said Tim, "if we do it, we'll come before the summer."

Out of sympathy and in spite of our own wishes, we tried to keep them from biting off more than they could chew, explaining to them that running a campsite can be rather intensive in high season, let alone combining it with giving birth. They treated it lightly and said they would ask some family members to come and help them. We didn't want to be pushy about it; after all, they were adults, and it wasn't their first child. Tim and Mara went back to the Netherlands, full of enthusiasm, but without committing to anything.

A week or so later, while an architect, sent by the father of the first couple's wife, walked around our property to make a detailed report of the real estate's condition, we were negotiating with Tim and Mara. In the first week of February, we reached an agreement. We were so happy! Would we really sell the campsite within three months? We made an appointment with the local notary to sign the preliminary contract the following week.

One night during that week, we came home after visiting some friends and saw a camper on our site. The signs at the entrance said we were closed, so what tourist in the world would be so desperate as to put his camper on our campsite? To our surprise, we identified him as the father of the first couple. He said he wanted to sojourn on the spot to get a better feel for it. We were so tired that we let him stay and went to sleep.

The next day he sat next to Jan on a bench outside, drinking a cup of coffee that we had offered him. After some informal small talk, he finally came to the point and said in a confidential tone, "I really like this place, but you have to lower the price a lot. You know, no one is ever going to buy it if you keep asking for that amount of money."

Jan really made an effort, but couldn't totally suppress the sound of triumph in his voice as he replied, "We have an appointment at the notary next week with another Dutch couple."

The look on the man's face went from astonished, then disappointed, to almost angry. Hadn't he instructed an architect to inspect our property? Didn't we think he was serious? It was the last time we saw him.

Actually, we had the appointment at the notary with Tim on Jan's fifty-third birthday. The notary was an impressive man, with a huge moustache that made funny movements every time he tried to pronounce the buyer's surname, which started with an *H*. He really did his best but, for French people, the aspiration just doesn't come naturally. It was as if he had a nasty hiccup and he slightly leapt up from his chair with every *H*. We had collected all the required documents so the rest went well, but it still took a couple of hours. After the long session, Tim went straight back to the Netherlands, eager to share the experience with his wife.

To celebrate Jan's birthday, we had invited friends for dinner that evening and wanted to seize the occasion to announce our big plans. Now that we had signed the contract, we could finally talk about it, but we weren't prepared for their reaction. They were shocked. They didn't share our enthusiasm at all. In fact, one friend even wept. "You've finally finished everything, and now you want to give it all away? Think about all the love you have poured into it! How can you leave just like that?"

They simply didn't understand. We tried to explain, but had to admit that even we didn't completely grasp why the desire to go to Italy was so strong.

We had agreed with Tim and Mara that we would try to transfer ownership by the end of May, just in time for them to receive the first tourists. Tim hoped that, by then, he would have overcome all financial hurdles concerning the buyout with his brothers. We were still wondering how they would manage with Mara's pregnancy, but they seemed to be confident and very sure about coming.

Anyway, we had at least three months to prepare our international move. We asked for quotations from moving companies and cleared boxes that we hadn't even unpacked after we had moved from the Netherlands. I began to learn Italian from the CD-ROMs I had bought and surfed the Internet to find a suitable correspondence course on art history. I didn't find one, but I ordered some beautiful books about the subject. Jan had started a quest on the Internet to find a church in Umbria. In France, we lived in the middle of a spiritual "nowhere." Only once a year, traditionally on Christmas Eve, we went to the nearest Protestant church, a forty-five minute drive away. The past year Jan had listened weekly to sermons that a pastor of a Christian church in Amsterdam published on the Internet. It had helped him grow in ways he never experienced before, so he felt it important to be able to attend a "real" church once we lived in Italy. For me it was all right, as long as we ended up in Umbria. Jan found a portal for Italian churches, but it didn't mention their locations. However, the website did have an email address, and Jan sent a short request for more information into anonymous cyberspace, praying that someone would read and answer it.

Two weeks later—the beginning of our patience training from which we would greatly benefit living in Italy—he received an answer with the email address of a Christian church in Perugia. Jan hadn't put any effort in learning Italian yet, so he wrote his next email in English, explaining our situation and his search, with the hope that the pastor would understand. Five days later, he received a friendly reply, in perfect English! The sender was Brad, an American missionary who attended that church. He invited us to get in touch as soon as we landed in Umbria. Jan took this as guidance from his Father; probably we needed to be close to Perugia, since this was the only church he had managed to find. But then he got in touch with a fellow Dutchman, a contact Brad had suggested to us. This man had served as a pastor in Brad's church, but had now returned to the Netherlands. His question was, "Why go to Perugia? God doesn't need you in Perugia, because He's already at work through several churches there!" Confusion crept in.

In the middle of the preparations, we also took time for sports to release the tension that was building. We ran in the woods and rode our bicycles around the lake, sometimes together, other times separately. If Jan went on his own, he often came back telling me that he had been preaching again. At first, I looked at him strangely. Preaching what? And to whom? He explained that he saw himself in front of many people in a church, and that words welled up in his mind, forming a sermon to tell the people about God's heart. It became so strong in him that he considered doing a Bible school to back up his renewed faith with a deeper biblical understanding. Although I didn't share Jan's convictions, for some reason I thought it would be good for him to do that.

In March, we decided that we needed to go to Italy to focus on the administrative side of our new life and attend to details such as applying for a fiscal code, establishing a bank account and, of course, looking for a house. This time, we didn't have the luxury of an animal sitter, so we decided that Jan would go alone. He would stay in the same B&B and work with the realtor we had seen in November. We sifted through their website once more to prepare a list of potentially interesting properties. We also contacted some other real estate agencies, and Jan made a few appointments. One of them, with the suggestive name *Inveni* (Latin for "I found it"), sent us a picture of a property with a brief description. It was huge, it was located in the woods close to Orvieto, and it looked very inhospitable. We responded that we weren't interested in that one, but kept the appointment for another house.

Before Jan departed, he visited a friend we had met recently—Peter, a Dutch retired pastor who lived in a small village at the foot of the French Pyrenees. Peter was a friendly, quiet man. He seemed at peace with the world, with himself, and with God, although he was visibly in deep pain, because he lost his wife less than a year ago. He claimed that God had let him know why he had called his spouse Home, but he still missed her tremendously. Through it all, he radiated a special kind of wisdom that had touched even my, unbelieving, heart. He listened to Jan talking about our desires, our plans, and our confusion. Jan also spoke about me and about my difficulties to believe.

At the end, Peter counseled, "It may not yet be easy for you to hear God's voice, but allow him to guide you. Pray, Jan, whenever and wherever you go in your search for a house in Umbria. Pray,

pray, and pray some more. Then follow his Spirit, because he will show you the way."

In addition, Peter gave him a book for me. Its title was *Challenge to Encounter*, and it discussed how one could approach some of the questions raised by philosophy and theology from a Christian standpoint. Peter explained, "Milly will open up to God through reading books."

When Jan came home, he gave me the book, a bit tentative. He explained that Peter had given it to him for me, but he did not tell me what Peter had said. I was outraged. "How dare you talk about me and about what I do or don't believe with someone I hardly know?"

Why did Jan meddle with my so-called spiritual condition at all? I was doing just fine! I didn't quite understand why I reacted so violently, but I flipped the book aside, convinced I would never read it. Of course, I was wrong.

The evening before Jan left for Italy, we talked about him house hunting on his own. To better target his search, we wrote a description of our dream house:

* It must be detached, ancient, built of natural stone, be in good condition (ready to move in), and have a floor surface of at least 2,000 square feet, excluding any annexes. We wanted independent guest rooms with a separate bathroom or an apartment for guests. We would

love to have a courtyard and a terrace with a view. All services, such as electricity, water, and telephone, must be present.

* Around the house, we wanted trees for shade and the possibility to create a vegetable garden of at least 2,000 square feet within close proximity to the house.

* The property must have at least 7-to-12 acres of land, with part of it woodlands so that we would have wood for our fireplaces, but mostly to use as grazing land for our horses. An olive grove, a small vineyard, and fruit trees should also be present or possible.

* The house must be situated in an environment with a shady forest nearby to walk with the dogs on hot summer days. To protect our dogs and cats, it must not be too close to a road with through traffic. It must lie within 3 miles of the nearest nice village with a bakery and no more than 30 minutes' drive from Perugia. We didn't want any noise from highways.

* The view must be wide, without visual pollution.

"I could never make a decision about a house on my own," Jan said after we finished the list.

"Well, first of all, it would be a real miracle if you find this house within a week," I replied. After our previous trip to Umbria, I doubted he would see anything that came close to fulfilling even half our requirements. "But anyway, I trust you. You're even more critical than I am!"

Jan wasn't convinced. "Only if you promise you will come over before we decide to make an offer."

I agreed without hesitation, sure that it wouldn't be necessary. I was wrong again.

CHAPTER FOUR

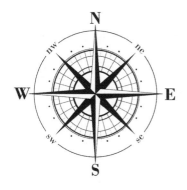

The House

*S*o on that grey and chilly day in March 2004, as I was carrying the logs for the stove into the kitchen, Jan was on his way to Umbria, Italy. Noticing that the further south he went, the sunnier and warmer it became, he delighted in this trip, although he had to drive more than six hundred miles in our uncomfortable four-wheel drive in one day. He arrived safe and sound, had a good night sleep, and awoke the next day ready for the hunt.

In the morning, Gregory took him to a few properties, each of them more disappointing than the other. Of course, Jan prayed all the way to and during the inspections. God didn't seem to say anything. In the late afternoon, Jan handled some administrative matters concerning the fiscal code, and the next day he had an appointment with the Inveni agency.

He found their office without problems and met Paolo, the owner, and Cristina, his secretary and translator. Because our list of requirements was so long, Jan limited himself to the most important ones: the house must be detached, away from busy roads, and have enough land for our horses. To Jan's surprise, Paolo said immediately, "I have your house!"

Curious, Jan asked for more information and was a bit frustrated when he realized that Paolo was referring to the same gloomy house near Orvieto we had already rejected. He began saying, "No, that is definitely not our house. We want to be near Perugia, not Orvieto!" However, as soon as he spoke the words, he felt something nudge at his thoughts and he remembered Peter's advice, "Follow his Spirit, because he will show you the way."

Disconcerted, Jan apologized for his negative reaction. "Uhm, wait, I'm sorry, can we go there anyway? On second thought, it might be interesting."

Paolo and Cristina looked a bit confused—yet another client who didn't know what he wanted. Nevertheless, they kept their composure, invited Jan into Paolo's car, and off they went.

The drive from their office, near Lake Trasimeno, to the house took about forty-five minutes, and the roadway passed beside beautiful cities such as Città della Pieve and Monteleone d'Orvieto, which clung fiercely to their hilltops in the bright spring sun. When they passed a small village with an ancient defense tower and a spectacular view over the valley, Cristina explained, "The property is in this municipality. Its name is Poggio."

Jan became more alert, expecting them to stop somewhere soon now, but they continued past Poggio. Jan spotted olive groves and vineyards as they followed the road that wound upwards. At the top of the hill, they left the asphalt to take a dirt road, which gradually went down again. Paolo drove his big car carefully, because the road was like Swiss cheese—full of holes. The views, on the other hand, were incredible. Woods and fields surrounded them, with a valley, rolling hills, and a walled hilltop city on the left. Finally, they took a right turn. At first trees and bushes blocked the view; then, halfway around a bend, the panorama opened up. Before them lay a deep valley with a glistening river, meandering amid lush forests. Paolo stopped the car and pointed in the distance, asking something in Italian.

"Do you see that huge rock?" Cristina translated, "That's Orvieto."

As they slowly continued around the bend, Jan tried to take in the overwhelming view through the side window.

Pointing his gaze again, he saw the property, which now appeared in front of the car. Destination reached! Amazed, Jan realized that the building and its surroundings didn't radiate the dark mood of the picture at all. The house had stone walls, pitched roofs with orange tiles, and he recognized the typical Umbrian architecture, where additions had been made to meet the needs of the farm families who had lived and worked there over the decades.

Paolo parked the car and they got out. Jan inhaled deeply to fill his lungs with clean air and stood motionless for a moment to soak up the environment. A choir of at least a dozen different birds welcomed him to the property, and the fragrance of sheer freshness entered his nostrils. Then he noticed that Paolo was motioning him to come, and together they walked around the house. Arriving at the other side, Jan couldn't believe his eyes. A courtyard! Between the right angle formed by two parts of the house and the stable on the opposite side, there was a little square with a blossoming apricot tree in the center.

Marveling, Jan followed Paolo and Cristina up an eight-step staircase and through a small portico into the house. It was filthy and full of old furniture, but Jan looked beyond all of that and saw the possibilities of creating our dream. The big open kitchen, the huge fireplace, the four spacious bedrooms, and the amazing view of the valley and Orvieto seemed perfect! Paolo and Cristina explained that the property did not contain just this one house; there was a second. The two houses, built back-to-back, had a total surface of more than 4,000 square feet, including the annexes. The surrounding grounds measured about 30 acres, with 12 of them pasture land, and the rest was woodland.

As they made a grand tour over the property, Jan found out that the second house was empty, not just of furniture, but also of services. Someone had started the renovation, but had gotten only the structural work done. Outside again, they tried to find their way to the pastures, dodging between brambles and wild fennel as the perfume of mint rose up from under their feet.

The land hadn't been maintained for over two years. The previous owner, who had lived in Rome but wanted to breed horses on this property, had died unexpectedly, taking his dream into the grave. The property had been for sale since his death, but no one had been interested enough to make an offer; this was odd according to Paolo, because it was beautiful and the price was reasonable. Some people had found it too isolated, while others had found it too large.

With growing wonder, Jan recognized that this property fulfilled almost all the desires we had included in our wish list; the short distance from Perugia and the terrace with a view were the only missing elements. Was this the place his Father wanted us?

Jan informed Paolo that he was truly interested. Paolo, in turn, promised to contact the widow of the previous owner and let him know her reaction. He suggested that, in the meantime, we made an offer, but Jan explained that before doing anything official he wanted me to see the property too.

In the evening, Jan called me and shared his amazement with me as he described what he had seen and heard. It really seemed as if this house was waiting for us.

"So why don't you make an offer?" I asked him.

"No, I can't without you!" he said and insisted that I prepare to come to Italy. He then promised to call me and confirm as soon as Paolo contacted him.

I spent all evening on the Internet trying to arrange a trip to Umbria. This wasn't easy at such short notice. Of course, I also googled *Poggio*, and the little bit of information I found was enough to make me daydream into the night before finally falling asleep.

The next morning, I waited for a phone call from Jan to go ahead with the flight reservation, but when he called, he had calmed down. The owner had said to Paolo that she wanted to talk with him first, and they had made an appointment for the next week. "So there's no rush," Jan told me, "and you don't need to come right now."

Although Paolo had repeated that we should make an offer, Jan had turned down his advice, relying on his "ex-businessman" point of view, convinced that our eagerness could possibly weaken our negotiating position. "I still have appointments today and tomorrow; maybe I'll see other properties that are worthwhile."

I accepted his decision, quietly hoping that he was right.

That evening he called again to give an account of another out-of-the-ordinary experience. He had been in a car with two real estate agents to visit a property that was interesting on paper, but they never made it to the house; they couldn't find it!

"We drove in circles for at least two hours! I was praying all the time and felt at peace about it, but the poor men were so embarrassed. At the end, when it got too dark to see the house anyway, I told them to forget it and assured them that it was no problem at all. They didn't understand, but I feel that it may have been my Father saying to forget about other houses, because he has already shown us the right one."

The next day, his feeling turned into certainty.

In the morning—I just had switched on the coffee machine and put some milk on the stove to make myself a nice mug of coffee—the telephone rang. The display showed an Italian number. I raised my eyebrows. *Why doesn't Jan call me on his cell phone?* But it wasn't Jan; it was Cristina from the Inveni real estate agency. At first, I didn't understand why she called, because a thick, charming Italian accent enveloped her English. Gradually, my comprehension grew, as well as the knot I felt tightening in my stomach.

"I cannot reach your husband," she said, "so I am calling you, because we have an urgent message for him. We have another person who is interested in the Poggio property, and he wants to make an offer."

I gasped. "But I thought that, for two years, no one had shown any interest?" I asked, while I considered the possibility that it might be a realtor's tactic to tempt us to make a premature offer. However, Cristina seemed honest enough.

"Yes, I know, and we are amazed too. Actually, this man is also Dutch. He came into our office on the same day as your husband. We went with him to Poggio in the afternoon. He really insists he wants to make an offer, but I explained to him that your husband has the first right to do that, because he was the first to visit the property."

I had never heard of that rule before; it surely did not exist in France or in the Netherlands, but I was thankful for it. Grabbing the milk from the stove, just before it bubbled over and burned, I promised Cristina that I would try to call Jan as well. Standing in front of the coffee machine, I dialed his cell phone several times before I finally contacted him.

Jan was visiting yet another property that morning, at the north of Perugia again, in a small village called Valfabbrica. It was a neat house, and it met many of our wishes, with everything seeming to be in good condition and, yet, it didn't light a fire in his heart. He listened politely as the estate agent explained the pros and cons of the property. When he answered his phone, he heard me shouting, "Where are you?" The agitation in my voice was evident.

"Why, what's going on?" was his surprised reaction.

"You need to go to Inveni to make an offer for the Poggio house as soon as possible! There's someone else who wants it too!"

When he hung up the phone, he told the agent that, unfortunately, he couldn't finish the inspection, because something urgent had come up. He ran to his car, phoned Cristina and told her he was on his way. During the journey to the office, he prayed. "Father, I'm so sorry that I didn't make an offer yet. I'm sorry that I still wanted to see other houses after you showed me the perfect one. Please forgive me and help us to buy this house, if that is your will."

He was convinced that he had taken a wrong turn in God's plan, and that the enemy of his soul and destiny was trying to block the way back by sending the other Dutchman.

It became a rather heated session in the Inveni office. While Paolo was preparing the necessary documents, the other Dutchman called. His name was Larry. He was angry with Paolo for not being able to make an offer. Cristina talked to him, because Larry didn't speak Italian. She managed to stay polite and explained patiently, several times, why they had given Jan the priority of making an offer. The phone call lasted almost half an hour. Relieved when Larry finally hung up, Jan tried to concentrate on Cristina's questions to get all data on paper.

Twenty minutes later, the phone rang again, and Larry's lawyer introduced himself to Paolo. *What? A lawyer? An Italian lawyer even? Wow, that man must really want the property.* Jan realized that Larry was getting on his nerves. For more than an hour Jan listened to Paolo, who explained the situation over and over again, all the while remaining very composed. Jan wasn't so calm, as his confidence in his Father's ways was put to the test. When he finally left the office, he felt like a wet rag, trying to mop up all the emotions that he had spilled. Nevertheless, the envelope he carried in his hand contained a signed and stamped copy of the official *proposta,* and the original was on its way to the owner in Rome.

"Father, thank you so much for your guidance. It's up to you now."

CHAPTER FIVE

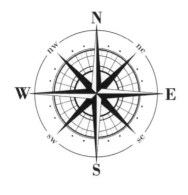

The Desire

While Jan sat in Paolo's office, I received a phone call that would change our life forever, although we would have to wait almost five years before the change arrived. My sister Elisabeth, eight years younger than me, called from the Netherlands. I thought that the timing was wonderful, because I really needed to share with someone what was going on. "We're about to buy a house in Italy!" I said, excited.

"What? But you're at home!"

I explained what Jan was facing in Umbria, and she understood my agitation. After we talked for a while about the situation, she changed the subject. "Actually, I'm calling because I have some news."

"Okay, tell me everything," I said, expecting something like another job or a new house.

Instead, she announced, "You'll be an aunt again in September."

I leaned against the kitchen counter as my mind stopped working for a few seconds. Then the full meaning of her words sank in, and my brain cells discharged with the rate of a machine-gun salvo. Like me, my sister didn't have children. She worked almost full time, as did her husband. They lived in a tiny house in a big city and worked mainly to afford long holidays in far-away places. We had talked with each other about creating a family, and she had always said that kids didn't fit their lifestyle. For various reasons, for me it had never been the right moment to have kids, and having a sister who didn't have them either was kind of comforting to me; it was like a bond between us.

"You're not pregnant, are you?" I asked, holding my breath but knowing the answer.

"Yes, I am," she said wryly.

At first, I felt betrayed. Hoping that she wouldn't hear my emotions through my voice, I managed an enthusiastic reaction, but then I experienced a tug, deep inside of me. Elisabeth's news was pulling the lid off some container I didn't even know was present. Now I saw it clearly: a huge gaping hole, filled to the brim with a desperate desire to have a baby. Without the lid, it overflowed, literally. Still talking with my sister, now about how the first three months of her pregnancy had been–nauseous–tears were streaming down my face. What was happening to me? The last thing I wanted to do was to embarrass Elisabeth or take away her joy, so I tried hard to hide my condition of utter confusion. However, I couldn't hold back one question. "Why? Why have you changed your mind?"

Carefully searching for the right words, she explained that our father's death had left her contemplating her frenetic life and wondering about its scope. She had realized that working and traveling weren't life-fulfilling. She wanted to do something "real and relevant." The result of her soul-searching was that she and her husband had decided to go for kids. "To counter the ugliness of death with new life and give my own life a purpose."

When we hung up the phone, I slipped down the cupboards onto the cold tile floor and cried, and cried, and cried. How was I supposed to handle this tsunami of emotions? Where did these feelings come from?

When my mind cleared a bit, I thought back to the times when I had seriously considered having children. The first time was with my previous husband, Dennis. We were both twenty-nine when we married, young enough to postpone any decision about children. In addition, I had a job; I was about to receive leadership responsibilities, and a child would interrupt my career path. However, seeing friends having babies, we toyed with the idea and, in my heart, it slowly grew into something that might become real.

One day, I bought him a little teddy bear as a playful way to introduce my serious desire. When I put it in his breast pocket, its little cuddly head appearing just above the edge, I looked into my husband's eyes expecting to see the same tenderness and love I felt in my heart. What I saw instead was harshness and refusal, almost panic. I felt hurt and humiliated. Taking the soft toy out of his pocket, I decided at that very moment never to mention the subject again.

What I didn't know was that Dennis carried a painful secret. At times, though, I had noticed something strange about him, especially on days after he came home late from some business dinner. It was as if he "shut down." I had no idea how to react to his behavior and, distressed, chose to ignore it. As soon as Dennis turned back to normal, we tried to carry on with marriage life as if nothing had happened. Eventually, he confessed a problem that had a huge impact on our relationship. He agreed to seek professional help but, at home, we kept avoiding talking about the situation. I built walls around my heart to exclude the hurt, but these same walls made it impossible for me to reach out to Dennis and support him in his struggle. In the end, he gave up on resolving the problem and said that he would never change. We decided to get a divorce. We had been married four years.

Two years later, I met Jan. The first evening we dated, he asked me whether I wanted children. He explained that he was happy with his two sons who were in their late teens, but that he would be ready for another kid if it were a strong desire of his future partner. Not allowing my feelings to get tangled up once more,

I remained aloof when I answered, "Well, I don't have a definite desire for a child. For me, it depends on the relationship; if it is good, and both the man and the woman want a baby, they should give it a try."

We didn't talk about it again until we were almost a year into our relationship, still living and working in the Netherlands. My period was late. The possibility of a pregnancy was filling me with joy, although I didn't dare to mention it to Jan, afraid to expose my vulnerability. Then one morning reality smashed my dream into little pieces, and while I sought comfort in Jan's arms, I shared my emotions with him, tears in my eyes. He looked at me, a bit puzzled. While he pulled back his arms, his words were distant. "You know we couldn't handle a kid, we both work full-time and, furthermore, I already have two boys."

His reaction was a stab in a wound that wasn't healed yet. Obviously, Jan was totally unaware of the impact of his reaction; he would never hurt me intentionally. But, for the second time in my life, I resolved not to bring up babies again, ever.

Later, in France, Jan said once or twice that having a baby would be the crowning touch to our relationship. However, he just mentioned it; he never talked about it directly, and neither did I. To me, the idea of a child as a crown was weird anyway. As if it was just the icing on the cake! I saw a child as the fruit, not as a decoration, of our marriage. Moreover, with a child would come the responsibility to plant, nurture, and foster the seed of the person that was enclosed inside that fruit. Anyway, I didn't want to relive the shattering of a dream, so I never gave it a serious thought. I just tucked it away. Now I knew where. And I also knew that I would have to bring up the subject once again, to share my feelings, my deep desire.

Could I handle exposing my heart and becoming vulnerable once more?

CHAPTER SIX

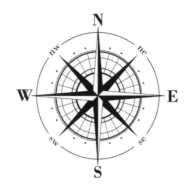

The Arrival

France, May 2004

The alarm sounded at 5:30 a.m. As soon as I woke up and turned it off, I was conscious of the mixed feelings inside me, fighting for priority. Excitement about the future we were about to step into, and nostalgia for the good things we would leave behind. Today was the day we would move to Italy.

Tim and Mara had arrived with their two small kids and her big, pregnant belly, and they were just as exhausted as we were. I had found it very disturbing to watch them settle into our house. Well, technically it was their house now, of course, since we had signed the final contract a couple of days before. Jan and I had agreed to stay two days longer to explain some of the ins and outs of the guest accommodation, because the first tourists would arrive within a week. This last night, we slept in the B&B room, because Tim and Mara had moved into our bedroom. I felt like a visitor in my own house, and that was certainly not a good feeling. It was time to go.

Jan was also awake, so we got up and dressed silently, not wanting to awaken the new owners. Tim and Mara had promised to say goodbye to us but, before we left, Jan and I wanted to take our last tour on *Domaine du Vieux Chêne*, just the two of us. Not only to walk the dogs, but also to say farewell to a huge chunk of our hearts.

Our three dogs greeted us with their usual enthusiasm, and we walked up the fields behind the house to a spot where we would have a view of the whole *domaine*. It was quiet outside, no sun, no wind, just grey clouds, as if nature was holding her breath in this special moment. Talking softly, we spoke of our feelings about the departure. I was ready to run away instantly, perhaps because I didn't want to see how other people appropriated this beloved piece of my life. Jan found it hard to leave and even shed a few tears as we stood hand in hand, taking in the wonderful view of our valley for the very last time. The little Shetland pony and the donkey, which we would leave with the new owners, stood calmly grazing in the valley. We hugged each other. The dogs played around us, ignorant of the big change that was about to happen in all of our lives.

"Okay, let's go," Jan said, finally letting me go, and we walked back toward the house.

Tim and Mara never woke up, so when we set off at 6:30, there was nobody to wave goodbye to us. However, I liked that, because now *we* would always remain the ones who said the last goodbye to other people on our *domaine*. While Jan drove us away, I looked around in the car to check one more time whether everything was okay for the long journey (over 600 miles) to Italy. Our three cats were in three benches, which we had stacked in the back of the car. I hadn't managed to administer them their tranquillizers (they didn't like traveling in a car), but I tripled their stress by trying anyway. In fact, I noticed that the most vigorous one, the only female, had already put a little paw through the bars, clawing around, in search of something to rip apart. The dogs, lying kind of draped around the pile of benches, remained cautiously out of her reach. Behind the car was a small trailer with our bicycles, two suitcases full of summer clothes, books, CDs, a CD player, and a few other indispensable items. We had put the rest of our belongings, more than 2,000 cubic feet, in a French storage facility.

Did I already mention that the house in Poggio had been taken off the market? In March, a week after Jan came home from Italy, Cristina had called us with the news that, for emotional reasons, the owner didn't want to sell the house now. She wanted to wait at least until the end of May, when her son would turn eighteen. Having reached adulthood, he could then try to get subsidies from the regional government to finish the renovation of the house. The news disconcerted us; we had to move out of our house at the end of May. We wanted to bring three dogs, three cats, and two horses to Italy and had no place to stay. In spite of the circumstances, Jan felt confident. "If My Father says 'A', he will also say 'B'," was his motto. I wasn't so sure. *Even finding a temporary address for our small zoo and ourselves will be a true miracle*, I thought.

Jan had called Peter again to share the details of his experiences in Italy in March, and Peter's advice had been simple: bless your enemies. At first, I thought it a bit odd; after all, these people didn't want to harm us personally, they were just pursuing their own interests. Jan explained that we could consider them spiritual enemies because they thwarted God's plan for our lives, but that God wanted us to bless them and love them anyway. Therefore, Jan blessed the owner and Larry, the other Dutchman who wanted to buy the house, daily and, occasionally, he involved me in the prayer.

On one particular evening, we were walking the dogs under a dark sky filled with millions of bright stars and an almost tangible galaxy spanning the heavens. Jan stopped and put his arms around me. Leaning my head against my husband, I looked up, wondering if it was really possible for one god to create such endless beauty. Jan prayed, "Dear Father, I bless the owner of the Poggio house. Please heal her heart and enable her to let go of the past, to let go of the house. I bless Larry. Please let him lose his interest in the house. I pray that he will find another property, another place to fall in love with. I thank you Lord that your yes is yes, always. In the meantime, please help us to find a place to stay in Italy. Amen."

I drifted away on the soothing sound of his prayer. Somehow, I felt that if that God of the universe existed, He surely could make a house available for us.

We hadn't heard from Cristina and Paolo again, but we chose to have confidence. One week before we left, the miracle happened. Via the realtors of the B&B in Umbria, where we started our Italian adventure in November, we found an *agriturismo* in a village close to Perugia. We, as well as our animals, were welcome to stay for at least a couple of months at a farm that offered tourist accommodation on the side. Jan was exultant. "You see what my Father can do?" he asked.

I wondered what kind of people would take in two horses, three dogs, three cats, and a homeless couple for a longer period.

The journey to Italy went smoothly, although the poor kitty never stopped clawing around, and one of the dogs hyperventilated all the way. We only stopped to refuel, to walk the dogs, and to swap places, taking turns driving. We didn't talk much. While the car consumed the road, one mile after another, we digested the transition of one life season to the next. There would be a financial change, because we had decided to live off Jan's pre-pension. We just hoped it would be sufficient until his real retirement at the age of sixty-five. The decision meant that we wouldn't be forced to develop a commercial activity; this was wonderful, because I was hoping that the new season would include a new life, which would, in itself, require a great deal of our time and energy.

When I had finally found the courage to share my intense emotions about my sister's pregnancy with Jan, including the eruption of the desire to have a baby too, he was amazed at first. He didn't have a clue that I was longing for a child, but then neither did I before my sister called. We had a long talk about the impact it would have on our lives, but he realized how important it was for me. We talked about his feelings and the expression he had used, "a child is the crown of our marriage." He explained that, of course, he didn't see a child as an ornament, but as a glorious celebration of our marriage. Eventually, in spite of our age and our history—after all, Jan had already two sons—he agreed: we would try to have a child. "If it is important for you, it is important for me. I want to see you happy," he said to me.

And happy I was! Although I hoped to conceive as soon as possible, I had already been disappointed twice in the past two months. Sometimes I got frustrated with myself. Why hadn't I allowed that seemingly bottomless pit, from which a now unstoppable stream of yearning surfaced, to be discovered sooner in life? Why had I allowed my hurt—my pride?—prevent me from talking with Jan earlier? Anyway, I daydreamed often about being pregnant. I melted whenever I saw baby clothes, I took my folic acid pills, and I often pictured myself with a beautiful big belly in a wide, white cotton dress on a terrace with a view.

After a long day of driving, we approached our temporary address in Italy around 8 p.m. We struggled to find the entrance and ended up on a dirt road, where the rain had carved deep trenches downhill. We were tired, the dogs were whining, and there we stood stuck in a downhill bend, with the trailer hanging at an odd angle behind the car. Jan didn't dare to continue, so he decided to get help. He put on the handbrake and got out of the car while I stayed with the animals.

I was relieved to see him come back ten minutes later. He was in the company of Vittorio, a tall, casually dressed man in his early forties, with a shaved head and an elegant, almost arrogant appearance. He didn't look much like a farmer to me, and the fact that he spoke almost flawless French further ruined his rural image. I had spoken with him once on the phone to get some information about the accommodation but, on that occasion, he had spoken very poor English. Anyway, he managed to coach Jan down the almost impassable road, and we finally made it to the farmhouse.

Vittorio showed us our one-room apartment, which was situated at ground level under the main house where he and his girlfriend Gabriella lived. It would be a challenge to live there with six pets for a long time, but at least it was spacious. It had some basic furniture: a couch, a kitchenette, a small table, two chairs, and a bed. The sight of the bed made me sigh with relief. During our phone call, I had asked Vittorio about the bed to know what size sheets to bring, and he had said it measured 47 x 67 inches. Oops! Jan and I love each other dearly, and we were looking forward to sultry summer nights, but there were limits. Our sheets would be large enough for sure but, to be on the safe side, we had also brought our camping mattresses and sleeping bags. Perhaps Vittorio's English was bad, he used a different unit of measurement, or he had just made an Italian guess at it; whatever the case, we were happy with a queen-size bed.

After we unloaded the car and the trailer, we opened a bottle of wine, raised our glasses to the safe arrival, collapsed on the big bed, and fell asleep as soon as our heads hit the pillows.

The next morning, we woke up later than usual. While Jan took a shower, I opened the big front door and stepped into the bright sunshine to explore our new environment. Low hills with scattered houses in the distance, a small forest and yellow wheat fields nearby—later, I learned it was actually spelt—an olive grove, and, right in front of our door, a huge lime tree with some plastic tables and chairs placed beneath. As soon as I noticed Vittorio coming toward me, I dove inside to get the box of presents we had brought: six bottles of the good French wine we had collected in the regions around our campsite for our guests to buy, and honey produced by the beekeeper who had his hives on our *domaine*. Vittorio seemed in a friendlier mood this morning. I asked him—in beginner's Italian—where we could walk the dogs, and he explained—in high-level French—how to get to a pond not too far away from the farmhouse.

"I'm going to walk the dogs!" I shouted to Jan.

I discerned an "okay!" through the sound of running water and called the dogs. An increasing volume of croaking frogs confirmed that we were proceeding in the right direction.

The pond was clearly artificial, because it had a precise rectangular form. Nevertheless, perhaps because its direct surroundings weren't maintained very well, it seemed to fit naturally into the landscape. Suddenly, our black lab plunged through the reeds into the water and swam as fast as she could towards something I couldn't distinguish right away. Squinting to have a closer look, I saw an animal that looked like an enormous rat! When it arrived close to the shore at the other side of the lake, with the dog fast approaching, the animal suddenly ducked. I expected it to reappear somewhere, but it never did. The dog swam in circles for a few minutes, confused as well, before giving up the search.

"Hey girl, that was a nice swim!" I exclaimed when she came back ashore.

She was still excited, alternating running around, rolling in the grass, and shaking the water out of her fur. Cold-water droplets hit my bare legs and made me shiver in spite of the warm sun.

When we came back to the house, I saw Vittorio again and told him what happened. "Ah, you met our nutria!" he exclaimed.

From his description, I understood it to be a cross between a rat and a beaver. I was enthusiastic; I had spotted my first species of Italian wildlife!

"No, you don't understand!" he replied, indignantly. "Nutrias are a real plague in Umbria, because their lodges destroy the shores of the farmers' water reservoirs for dry summers."

Shaking his head at my ignorance, he walked up the stairs to his front door and disappeared inside.

Meanwhile, Jan had set one of the plastic tables and improvised a breakfast: two apples, two candy bars, and two mugs of lovely-smelling coffee. Among the indispensable items we had brought were a real Italian cafetiere and a milk foamer. We sat down, in the midst of six pets cautiously exploring their new environment, and enjoyed.

During our first week at the farm, we just tried to settle in. Jan immediately embraced the Italian practice of taking a siesta after lunch. At first, I experienced a rush of adrenalin, in spite of the stress of the last period in France, or maybe because of it. As the day revealed that the ease with which Vittorio and Gabriella accepted a couple and eight animals reflected in not bothering too much about dirt, I invested all of my excess energy in a cleaning marathon. Two days later, our new abode was spick and span, and I finally relaxed as well. The only other thing we accomplished was enclosing Vittorio's olive grove with an electric fence to prepare it for our horses, who would be arriving the next week.

When we felt rested enough to begin exploring the area, we had our first cultural experience. In a local supermarket, I had found a flyer that announced an outdoor concert of classical music in Pietrafitta, a village about twenty minutes away. It touted free access, so it offered a real opportunity for these two Dutchies abroad! We imagined ourselves in the romantic atmosphere of a medieval village, the sound of sweet strings caressing our ears in the soft summer air, stars sparkling above our heads… Well, we should have known better had we read who sponsored the evening: the national electricity company. To make a long story short, we found ourselves literally in the shadow of two huge, smoking cooling towers of a power plant, where the thin sound of music almost completely faded away before it reached the audience. After the first piece, we left, quivering in the cold wind. Back in the apartment, we laughed at our naiveté and made ourselves a nice cup of tea to get warm again.

Vittorio and Gabriella, as we soon figured, weren't traditional farmers; they produced ecobiological products and were politically active as members of a small, local left-wing party. This year they grew spelt and tomatoes. We also discovered, close to the irrigation pond that housed the nutria, a recently constructed, fully equipped olive oil production plant. It seemed obsolete though, hardly accessible through the bushes that grew all around it, with heaps of olive pulp from some previous harvest rotting away next to the building. When we asked Vittorio about it, he answered nonchalantly, "Oh yeah, we built that a couple of years ago, but we didn't make enough money with the oil, so we quit." Every now and then, we found Vittorio sitting inside a metal frame. He explained to us that the energy of the universe converged on the top of the frame and entered into his being, creating a balance between the physical and the spiritual.

Of course, in that first period in Umbria, we contacted Cristina to know more about the house we were waiting for. She told us that the owner had scheduled a meeting with Paolo on June 20 to let him know whether they would sell the property. This news, however, didn't hold us back from visiting the house. I loved every square inch of it. As we strolled in and around the house (we had gotten in through an open window), we dreamed aloud. "Kitchen here, bedroom there, nursery…"

CHAPTER SEVEN

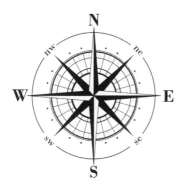

The Acquaintance

*W*e did it! Proud and relieved, we looked at the long-awaited documents in our hands: stamped copies of our requests for residence permits with the statement that we could collect the permits on September 7.

Armed with passports and photographs, we had gone to the *Questura*–the Italian national police force offices–in Perugia, which also housed the aliens' office. According to European regulations, we, as Dutch citizens, didn't need such permits at all, but it takes time to implement a European law. On Monday at 8:30 a.m., we went to the end of a line with at least a hundred other foreigners, waiting for the office to open. I would do the talking; thanks to my CD-ROM study, I spoke Italian better than Jan did.

Unfortunately, that day we didn't make it past the first obstacle: the porter's lodge. The lodge's windows were so high that we had to look up at the uniformed porter. Perhaps to reinforce the authority of the person who was now looking down on us? The officer was a stern-looking woman who, after I had explained our request in my best Italian, snapped, "*Domani!*"–"Tomorrow!" She didn't explain why, nor could she tell me whether we had to bring other documents.

The next morning, same time, same place, similar line, we found indeed another porter when we finally reached the lodge's window, a man this time. Luckily, this porter didn't only say, "*domani*". When I asked what other documents to bring the next day, he referred us to his colleague who was sitting in the same lodge behind another table and had another long line of people waiting in front of the window. No problem; having read *The Dark Heart of Italy* by Tobias Jones, we were prepared to stand in line an average of two hundred hours a year. Moreover, in the midst of so many people of different nationalities, hearing so many languages, we didn't get annoyed at all. When we reached the window again, we found the police officer there was almost friendly. He even jotted down a list of required documents to bring the next day, again at 8:30 a.m.

Wednesday morning we were successful. We completed our waiting time, went past the porter's lodge, waited some more, were admitted inside the office to the end of another line and, finally, arrived at the counter, triumphantly shoving our documents towards the police officer on duty. The first thing he said was that the documents weren't sufficient. Disconcerted, I showed the piece of paper with his colleague's scribbles to convince him that they were. He called the *capo*–the boss–obviously not wanting to take the responsibility of admitting these strangers into Italy. They discussed, I tried to explain, they discussed again, and then the boss gave us forms to fill out. When we had completed the forms, we lined up once more and the police offer called his boss one more time to check the forms. Then he finally surrendered and handed us the copied request. It was ten o'clock in the morning; the ideal time of day to have a cappuccino and a cream croissant–*cornetto*–in the nearest bar.

Nothing could, and nothing ever would, stop us from loving Italy and its people, despite the fact that two days later, the triumph of the first successful step to settle in Italy lost a bit of its luster. Cristina called to give us the news that the owner of the Poggio house had postponed her decision until July. Her son needed more time with the region to request the necessary subsidies.

Paolo was a bit embarrassed about the owner's behavior, and his sympathy for us shone through as he proposed that he show us another property. We didn't want to disappoint him, so we let us drive to a beautiful spot on a hill on the boundary of Tuscany, with a view of the city of Chiusi, enough land for the horses, three hundred(!) olive trees, and a ruin. The whole lot, however, came with a high price. We declined politely. Jan shared with Paolo how his faith made him believe that the Poggio house would become available. As he spoke, Paolo looked at Jan with a mix of amazement and respect. When Jan finished talking he said, "I admire your confidence, but we must remain realistic."

"I am," Jan replied, "my Father is very real."

Paolo smiled, but didn't answer. I felt a bit awkward about my husband witnessing to someone we hardly knew.

We also had an appointment with Brad, the American missionary who Jan had contacted while we were still in France. We met at the train station in Perugia. Brad was a short, chubby man, with a beard and friendly eyes behind thick glasses. While we walked to a bar and had coffee, Jan did almost all the talking. I just listened as the two men chatted about their faith and their backgrounds. Brad and his wife had come to Italy more than fifteen years ago to set up a Christian ministry aimed at relieving the psychological suffering of ill people in hospitals, by sharing the love of Christ with them.

Brad's words, explaining the beauty of his work, touched a sensitive spot in my heart. Memories of my father's agony on his sickbed flooded my mind, and it was as if something shifted my point of view. Studying art history all of a sudden seemed futile and purposeless; I wanted to spend my time at something more relevant. Feeling slightly puzzled and not having a clear picture of the alternatives, I heard Brad invite us to come to the next Sunday morning service and to lunch at his house afterwards. Jan happily accepted. I agreed mainly to satisfy Jan, with many questions in my heart.

That Sunday we drove around the outskirts of Perugia, looking for a building that could serve as a church. Brad had given us the address and, after we spotted somebody to ask—not many people were on the streets on Sunday morning—we finally pulled into the parking lot of an apartment building. It should be the right location, but we still didn't see a church or any churchgoers. When we called Brad on his cell phone to check, he said, "Don't move; we'll be there in five minutes!"

Another car pulled in, and a well-dressed couple stepped out. Then a car with a young family arrived. They greeted one another and, gradually, more people began to gather on the parking lot, casting curious glances our way. We noticed a big car coming, with two adults and four children, with ages ranging between eight and sixteen. Brad, his wife Sandra, their daughter, and their three sons had arrived. They welcomed us with big smiles. Brad introduced us to the other people, and every person shook hands with us, welcoming us with the friendly greeting, "*Pace.*"

I felt out-of-place, almost as if it was written on my forehead, "I don't believe in God." One of the men walked to a grey metal garage door on the ground floor of the apartment building, unlocked it and, while it opened with a lot of noise, we saw the entrance of the church appear. Five minutes later, we sat in a big room on the first row of chairs—no pews—between Brad and Sandra, feeling as though we were their protégés.

Behind us, the room slowly filled up with about fifty people. In front of us, a man took up a guitar, while others positioned themselves behind a keyboard and a drum set. Three women, who had covered their heads with a small veil, picked up microphones. A man in his early forties, dressed in a suit, stood discussing something with the keyboard player. I didn't know what to expect and watched the activity with a mix of apprehension and curiosity. Then the man in the suit stepped onto the pulpit; obviously, he was the preacher. He spoke a few phrases to welcome the people, prayed something in Italian I didn't quite follow, and then the music began.

With the first notes of the song, something softened inside of me. A joy welled up, and warmth melted away the worry. This music, this song, brought something to the atmosphere that I didn't understand. I found myself singing, with all my heart, the words that were projected on the wall, "My Jesus, my Savior, Lord there is none like you; All of my days, I want to praise the wonders of your mighty love…"

Before long, I noticed tears were streaming down my face. Oh my, what was happening here? Why was I crying? Embarrassed, I looked at Jan from out of the corner of my eye and saw him wipe away a tear as well. I didn't have a clue what was going on, but it certainly felt good and left me wondering throughout the service.

Later, during the simple but substantial lunch at Brad and Sandra's, I remained pensive while listening to their story. Their words further added input to my reflections. "We live off little money, but every time we really need something, we pray about it and see that God is faithful," Brad said, and added, "He even gave us a car!"

Jan told them all about how and why we came to Italy and ended with, "So here we are, but we don't know what God wants us to do!"

"Don't worry," replied Brad, "he'll show you when you need to know. For now, take the time to learn Italian, because you can't be useful for God in Italy if you don't speak the language."

Jan, wavering, agreed; he did not have a gift for languages and dreaded the prospect of wasting a lot of time trying to speak Italian before getting to the real job. I, on the other hand, cheered silently; I love languages and I love to learn them well.

Before we left their house, Sandra asked me whether I liked to read. When I responded positively, she gave me a book. It was a Christian novel, but I couldn't refuse her friendly gesture.

Brad's words about learning Italian encouraged us to complement our growing practical language skills with some theoretical schooling. We decided to enroll in an intensive Italian course at the *Università per Stranieri*–the University for Foreigners–in Perugia. It required that we attend the school for the entire month of July, twenty-seven hours a week. Because Jan hadn't done the self-study as I had, we started at different levels, and with different schedules. With just one car and temperatures in the nineties, we spent many sticky hours in Perugia, either sitting in classrooms without air conditioning or strolling in a sweltering city.

Apart from discovering that I still wasn't pregnant, three emotional moments interrupted the stringent rhythm of getting up at 6:30 a.m., walking the dogs, driving to Perugia, studying, driving back to our apartment, walking the dogs again, cooking, eating, and sleeping. The first moment was early in July, when my brother called with the news that Mom had been diagnosed with a heart condition and was now on the waiting list for open-heart surgery. The second occasion presented itself on July 23, when my brother-in-law called to tell us that Elisabeth had given birth to a son, two months early. The third interruption was almost a week later, when Cristina called to tell us that the Poggio house was for sale again, and the owner wanted to meet us during the first week of August. There was a major setback though: the asking price had gone up 60 thousand dollars.

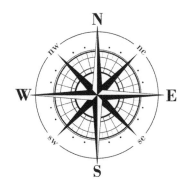

CHAPTER EIGHT

The Search

O n the first Sunday in August, I cried again in church. Of course, the pastor saw it, because we still sat on the first row between Brad and Sandra. At the end of the service, he asked if anyone wanted to come forward to give his or her heart to the Lord. I knew he was referring to my blubbering, assuming that God had touched me. However, this time my tears didn't come from some spiritual joy. I was hurting and angry with God, although I still didn't know whether I believed in him. Maybe I doubted his existence more than ever.

My tiny, premature nephew was in trouble. During a routine check of the baby, a doctor had discovered that he had a large tumor in the central part of his brain, which would eventually cause his death. My sister and her husband were devastated. So was I, not understanding why a loving God would allow that little child and his parents to suffer. I was filled with unbelief and frustration, and yet I prayed to him, "If you exist, and if every person is entitled to one miracle in a lifetime, then please let my miracle happen for this boy."

The pastor waited in vain for me to come to the front as I sat with my head bowed, watching my hands fidgeting with a paper handkerchief, trying to stop my tears of dismay.

After the first time in June, we had continued to attend church on Sundays. Every week at least one of the songs made me cry and, each time, we grasped more of the pastor's message as our Italian improved. Furthermore, I made a big step; I read Sandra's book. In the beginning, I read skeptically, with hesitation, but as I progressed in the story about a woman who, in the midst of difficulties, found God through loving people around her, I began to like the book. When I gave it back to Sandra, she offered me another one. This time I felt less embarrassed. The title of the book was *The God Chasers*, and it told about real people going after intimacy with a living God. Gradually, something changed in my attitude towards faith. It felt as though my mind opened up to the possibility of the supernatural. I was willing to admit that maybe, just maybe, there was something more than met the eye.

My studies in psychophysiology, which I concluded when I was twenty-six, had left me with a kind of what-you-see-is-what-you-get portrayal of humanity. "If you can't measure it, it doesn't exist." Each person's life, including all so-called psychological experiences, was just a more or less complicated interaction of internal, physiological processes and external stimuli. The evolution of the species was an accomplished fact, and moral behavior was the result of evolving social life, a kind of survival of the fittest group. People, as highly evolved beings, were capable of self-reflection and could experience positive emotions, including enjoying beauty, love, and happiness, but in the end, everything just aimed at the procreation of species. Taking stock of the pointlessness of individual life, I had decided to go for the positive emotions, so that at least I had a personal goal to pursue. I would be useless, but happy.

There had been a short period in my life though, in which I had at least tried to believe. I was almost sixteen when my best friend, Chrissie, died in a car accident while she and her first boyfriend were walking hand in hand along the road, under a starry night. The driver was drunk and never saw them until the car hit them. She died on the spot. Her boyfriend was badly injured, but lived. Chrissie's death shocked me and rocked all securities in a phase of life that is insecure enough in itself.

Shortly before the accident, Chrissie had joined a local Youth for Christ group and, partly because I couldn't accept that she would be gone forever, partly out of a desire to keep her alive through continuing what she had begun, I visited the same group. I met about ten friendly young people, between fifteen and twenty-five years old, who told me that Chrissie was in heaven now. They prayed for me, and we read the Bible. I bought my own Bible, an easy-to-read version, and I liked the Gospels. A real adolescent, I experienced a sort of romantic affinity with what I read, and I wrote poems about Jesus' love and care. The Old Testament, on the other hand, was a gloomy book to me. I found it was full of wrath and wars, and difficult to fathom.

I liked the Youth for Christ group, and I even "gave my heart to Jesus" during a huge national Christian youth event, but I guess I never really understood what it meant. I also found it hard to believe in creation as narrated in the book of Genesis and somehow felt that, if I didn't trust the Biblical basis of life, it would make me a hypocrite to say that I believed the rest.

At the age of seventeen, I had my first serious boyfriend. He was an atheist, and I left the Youth for Christ group. My life headed in a completely different direction.

We were in our last year of high school and living in the seventies. Perhaps the sixties still had a cute wholesomeness, with flower power and "all you need is love," but now it was just the raw thing. Anything must be possible. I found out that, to have a relationship in which I hoped to find romance and love, there was a price to pay. Unquestioning, I just went with the flow.

On Saturday evenings, I went to the disco, and a bartender kept offering me free glasses of vodka-orange. I was very insecure about my looks and my behavior. To my surprise, I lost my shyness after a drink, so I drank more. I loathed my parents' rule to be home at midnight but, looking back, I think it saved me from lapsing into an alcoholic coma more than once. I had always been a good student at school, but I stopped working and, through sheer luck, managed to pass the exams anyway.

During my university years, I discovered that my relationships didn't fulfill the desire to love and be loved unconditionally, to be someone's Number One. Instead, I found out how it feels to be betrayed, and how easily love gives way to jealousy, distrust, and resentment. Strong, destructive emotions that didn't disappear at the end of a relationship, but were passed on to the next.

Then I met Dennis through mutual friends during a holiday. We fell head over heels in love and decided to marry within a year. Four years later, we divorced. It left me wounded, and bitterness continued to grow in my heart.

In the meantime, I had finished my studies and decided that I didn't want to work as a psychophysiologist. Instead, after I completed a post-academic computer programming course, I started a career with an international IT company. There I found out that I didn't like full-time programming at all, so I looked for a job in which I would find more satisfaction. I became a technical writer, a profession I really liked. But, soon, a lack of challenge spurred me to accept a management role and, still later, a job in external communication.

In my early thirties, single again, I was an obvious target for married men in their mid-life crisis looking for an adventure. I wasn't in search of simple distractions; I was still looking for real love, unconditional love, to overcome my lack of self-confidence and give a purpose to my life. Yes, I made mistakes. In the beginning, I simply denied what it was doing to me but, at a certain point, I decided that it was time to see a psychologist. I felt not only useless, but also used, confused, and extremely unhappy. Without a real love in my life, a man who made me his first priority, I was worthless, not being able to enjoy anything. Things that normally filled me with joy, such as the beauty of nature or music, only added to the emptiness. I registered them, but didn't experience them. I was living life at a distance.

The psychologist told me that my happiness shouldn't depend on other people and assured me that my identity didn't hinge on what happened to me. I had to look into myself, identify who I was, and what were the qualities that made up my personality. Using my talents for what were, at least in my eyes, relevant causes, would contribute to my happiness. Well, that was easier said than done. My professional responsibilities had increased, but didn't give me fulfillment either. With more study, aiming for another career step, I tried to bridge the gap to what I thought would finally grant self-realization. Sometimes I felt like a wandering sheep, always searching for the greener grass.

Spending more time at work and study, meeting no new people at all, but still longing for the love of my life, I took the plunge and put an ad in a newspaper. "Cheerful woman, 35, keen on outdoor sports, looking for a friend between 27 and 45, non-smoker, to share sporting activities."

Jan's letter was among the twenty-plus responses I received. Why did I select his? It was short, to-the-point, stating that he was divorced with two teenage boys, that he traveled a lot for his work, and always carried his running shoes with him. In addition, there was this one phrase that said, "I have some dear friends." The sensitivity in the words "dear friends" struck me; if a man could feel that much of affection for friends, maybe he would be capable of really loving me.

After a phone call—he had a beautiful voice—we made an appointment in a restaurant. There was an instant affinity between us. The waitress had to come back four times to take up our order, because we just couldn't stop talking. When we finally had determined what to eat, it turned out we had chosen the same dish, roasted salmon. That first evening, Jan told me he was a Christian and asked me whether that was a problem for me.

"No, not at all. People are free to believe in whatever they want. I respect your faith," I answered. *After all, nobody is perfect*, I thought.

The first two years of our relationship, while we were still in the Netherlands, we both had busy jobs and didn't see each other often. Jan hardly ever mentioned his faith and, frankly speaking, I didn't notice much of it either. Then we made the life-changing decision to give up our careers and start a campsite in the south of France. We got married two weeks before we left the Netherlands in 1998.

To Jan it was important to marry in church. I agreed, obviously not for religious reasons, but because it gave our marriage a security line. Jan would vow to be a good and reliable husband before his Father, not just to me. We met the pastor who would marry us some time before. He was a friendly, older man. I don't know whether he realized that I wasn't a believer, but he made me feel comfortable. I even asked him to pray that my father, who was already ill, would be able to visit us in France. However, the moment he proposed that we kneel down during the nuptial vow, I felt reluctance rise within me. Bowing my knees before a god I repudiated would be the pinnacle of hypocrisy. It would make my wedding a theatrical performance, and I wanted it to be real. Luckily, Jan understood when I explained to him afterwards, and he called the pastor to tell him we would remain on our feet. The ceremony was simple, with just family and a few friends, but it felt sincere. Our honeymoon was the emigration.

We had been looking forward to our new lives, but the first year in France was difficult. Suddenly, we found ourselves in the middle of nowhere, together 24/7, attempting to work as a team to set up a campsite from scratch. Family, friends, and acquaintances from the Netherlands all wanted to explore our new place and, after having driven nine hundred miles, enjoy a holiday on our property. Jan and I needed time alone to grow in our marriage, but it seemed there was always somebody around. I didn't feel cherished. Jan got offended. We had many shouting arguments, stopped only because someone walked into the room, leaving us with little time to talk it over. We said ugly things to each other and we were miserable.

Somewhere at the end of that first year, Jan felt he should deepen his faith. He dug up two books: one that had been his mother's, containing meditations about a loving God, and another that his father had given him, *Solving Life's Problems* by Yong-Gi Cho. He kept a Bible on his bedside table and read it every night while waiting for me to come to bed. In the beginning, he tried to involve me, but he learned quickly that trying to convince me about God didn't work. The harder he pushed, the further away I ran. If he suggested that we read the Bible, I went looking for books of Carl Jung. The idea that he prayed for my conversion made me furious. I respected his convictions, so why couldn't he do the same with mine? In the end, he gave up talking to me about his faith. He just continued to live it.

While he dived deeper, I saw him slowly change. Our arguments became less intense, because instead of letting it escalate, Jan was able to say, "Yes, you're right. I'm sorry. I'll try to change that." The first few times I felt triumphant; I had won another battle! However, later I began wondering what was happening to Jan. Sometimes he shared that he had been praying to his Father for something and afterwards told me how his prayers had been answered. Often I got irritated with him, thinking it was just a coincidence. Other times, he would come back after a run in the woods, radiant, because the Holy Spirit had told him to modify this or that in his thinking or behavior. He was gradually being transformed, as if a huge hand was molding him, bit by bit, day by day. Amazed, I watched how the proud former businessman humbled himself by admitting his mistakes and being open to change and, above all, by sharing it all with me.

Every now and then, I wished I could have his faith, that I could see his Father as my Father but, usually, my pride and my bitterness stood in the way of even considering it. I didn't need some extraterrestrial power to live my life! I did wonder, though, where the feeling that something crucial was missing in my life came from. That awkward longing for the undefined, which I had tried to fulfill with relationships, work, sports, and knowledge, had never disappeared. Even coming to France, living in the midst of nature, a dream I had always cherished while working in air-conditioned offices during my business career, didn't give me the sense of accomplishment I had expected.

Now, five year later, in Italy, at the age of almost forty-three, I found myself going to church and reading Christian books. Sometimes, when Jan was out of sight–I was far too proud to admit it–I even read a chapter in the Bible. In addition, I began reading Peter's book, *Challenge to encounter*, although keeping that top secret. However, this particular Sunday I was only angry that the God whose existence I was investigating apparently had allowed a tumor to grow in my sister's newborn son.

When I spoke to my sister a few days later, she was extremely relieved, because another doctor had a look at the X-ray and said that he didn't understand why the first doctor had seen a tumor; he didn't see anything at all! Understandably, Elisabeth was furious with the first doctor, who had let them worry an entire weekend for nothing. During the telephone call, I fully agreed with her, and we grumbled together at so much ignorance.

After we hung up the phone, a thought crossed my mind and left me motionless for a long moment. *Could this be the once-in-a-lifetime, life-saving, divine miracle I have been asking for?*

CHAPTER NINE

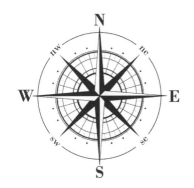

The Answer

August 2004

"It's like wanting to buy a ship without having the money for the sails," the older man said to us.

We sat in the Poggio house around a table with Paolo, Cristina, Dariella—the owner of the house—her brother, and her parents. We had been talking for at least an hour about the house, Dariella's situation, our horses, and our background, mixing business with social talk. It had been an animated discussion in a friendly atmosphere. Paolo and Cristina did most of the talking, but Dariella and her family seemed fairly open towards us. She especially liked the idea of horses on the property, so that a small part of the dream of her late husband would live on.

Then serious business began. Paolo had told them that we didn't want to pay the increased price, but that we would stick to the offer we had made in March. We filled them in on our financial situation; paying the higher price would leave us with too little to afford the renovation, even if we did it ourselves. Now Dariella's father, a man with a neatly trimmed white beard, looked sternly at us through his glasses, waiting for our reaction to his statement.

Paolo replied for us with a friendly smile, but with a straightforward response, "Maybe the ship is too expensive."

Her father grumbled something I didn't understand, and Dariella suggested that we all take five days to think it over. "I like you both and I would love to sell it to you. I'm sure that we'll find a solution, if you just reconsider your offer."

When we said goodbye, the father said in a confidential tone to Jan that he was on our side, because he thought it was time for his daughter to let go of her husband's past. "By the way, your wife has beautiful blue eyes," he added.

At these unexpected words Jan looked first at me, wide-eyed and speechless, and then looked back at the father, whereupon the man told Jan that he, too, had beautiful eyes. So the meeting ended on a positive note.

Jan still prayed every day for Dariella, blessing her with all his heart. He now also asked for wisdom concerning the new bid we should make. We talked a lot about it and felt it would be reasonable to increase our offer, but to no more than the original asking price. Confident and at peace with our decision, we called Cristina so that she could prepare the official documents. She then told us the startling news: Dariella had informed them that she had an appointment the next day with Larry, the Dutchman who had tried to make an offer on the same day as Jan back in March. He had contacted her directly, without the agency. This would make his offer more attractive, because neither of them would have to pay the realtor's fee. Our minds reeled upon hearing this news, and our patience and empathy for Dariella's emotions concerning the sale of her husband's dream dwindled.

Cristina shared our feelings. "However, we can't change the situation. All we can do is wait and see," she said.

"And pray," Jan finished her sentence.

After the phone call, Jan prayed and blessed both Dariella and Larry again. His confidence was further put to the test.

The next day, to take our minds off the house, we accepted the invitation of Vittorio and Gabriella to join them and some friends to visit Gubbio, a city in the north east of Umbria, about an hour's drive. It hosted a jazz festival, and we were going to attend an open-air concert in the evening. This time we made sure that it would be in the historic center… and it turned out to be a wonderful trip.

We arrived in the late afternoon and had our bicycles with us to explore Gubbio's surroundings. While we cycled through the gently sloping landscape, we were reminded of the beauty of our home in France, that is, if we averted our gaze from the mountaintops of the Apennines rising in the east. Before long, Jan and I left the Italians behind us. Pedaling, panting, and perspiring between pastures and cypresses, we exchanged sweet memories of the past and speculated about the future that remained unsure. But when you're surrounded by lovely scenery in one of the most awe-inspiring countries of the world, who frets about anything?

When we returned to the car, we rinsed with a bit of water that we had brought in bottles, changed our clothes, and went into Gubbio to discover its beauty. The city is built on terraces on the slopes of Mount Calvo, and the narrow streets exuded a medieval atmosphere. The *Piazza della Signoria*, with the *Palazzo dei Consoli*, particularly impressed us—a huge square that formed a kind of balcony, overlooking the lower part of Gubbio and the green landscape around it. The *palazzo*, built in the 14th century as the community hall, now housed a museum.

Later, sitting at a long table outside a small restaurant in the *Via dei Consoli*, we ate pizza in the company of the group of friends. While the Italians talked with one another, we were fascinated by their apparent capacity for multi-tasking. Between bites of pizza and sips of beer—most Italians drink beer only when they eat pizza—they were talking with loud voices and gesticulating with both hands, but they didn't wait their turn. They just all talked at the same time. Could they really listen and talk simultaneously? Although Vittorio still wanted to speak only French with us, we realized that our Italian had greatly improved in the almost three months that we had been immersed in Italy. However, that evening, as we tried to follow what was being said, our brains shut down. With the whole setting being so Italian, we simply decided to enjoy the sounds of the language without bothering about our lack of understanding. After we finished the pizza, we moved to the picturesque *Piazza Bosone* to listen to the music. A great ice cream from the *gelateria* on the *piazza* made the perfect ending to our day.

We didn't hear anything from the real estate agency for a week. "Wait and see," seemed to become the motto of August, as if the summer heat was slowing everything to a snail's pace. In addition, my thoughts had turned to my mother, who was on the waiting list for heart surgery. We hoped they would call her up soon, because she was constantly struggling with her shortness of breath. I planned to fly over to assist her as soon as I knew the date, but the hospital said there were many cases even more urgent than hers, so they kept delaying the operation. "Wait and see." I found it difficult to wait, because I also desperately wanted to visit my sister and see her son, but our new budget required combining the two occasions into one trip.

Then one day, Jan received a phone call from his nephew Paul, who worked as a surgical assistant in the cardiac department of a hospital in Amsterdam. Earlier that week, we had updated friends and family by mail about our Italian adventure, and had also shared the reasons for my upcoming stay in the Netherlands. Paul, now in his forties, had been a Christian since his teenage years and had always been very frank about it. Although backsliding every now and then, deep in his heart he always remained a big Jesus fan. After the formalities, Paul said, "I read your email about Milly's mother and her operation. You know, where I work I hear rumors about other hospitals. It seems that the cardiac department at the hospital where she's on the waiting list doesn't have a good reputation."

"Wait!" Jan replied, "I'll put you on the loud speaker so that Milly can listen."

When I heard what Paul said as he repeated his message, my heart dropped. Mum needed that operation badly, and I was aware of the risks it entailed at her age—eighty-one—but now I became seriously worried. So soon after my father died, I didn't want to lose my mother as well because of an operation team that didn't function well.

Fortunately, Paul had also good news. "In my hospital, there is a very competent heart surgeon. He's a Christian. If you want, I can ask him if he wants to operate on your mother."

My heart lifted. "Yes, please, if you can do that, I'll be so grateful!" I shouted into the telephone that was still in Jan's hand.

"Okay," Paul continued, "however, the one thing I can't guarantee is the timing. I don't know this surgeon's schedule, but the sooner you decide, the sooner we can get things going."

I explained to Paul that I would have to talk with my brother and sister before deciding. He understood my reasoning and said that he would wait for my answer.

So this was the dilemma: have my mother operated on quickly in a hospital by a team with a questionable reputation, or have her operated on some indefinite time later by a Christian surgeon in a hospital recommended by Jan's nephew. Both my sister, who obviously had other things on her mind, and my brother said they left the decision up to me. While they were upset about the bad news, they were hesitant because they didn't know Jan's nephew.

"Wait and see," wasn't going to solve the problem; I would need to decide. I was pulled towards Paul's option, which seemed the safest one, but the morning I was going to share this choice, my brother called me with news that cast doubt on the whole situation. The first hospital had an opening the week after next. Now what should I do? Cancel it?

That afternoon I spent several hours in an Internet/telephone café in Perugia, phoning doctors of the first hospital to know more, inquiring of the Dutch National Health Service about the possibility of changing hospital, mailing Paul and my siblings, looking up flights and prices, and trying to organize all the information in order to make a well-grounded decision.

My head felt full and heavy as I walked back to the car, which I had parked just outside the historical center. At that hour in the early evening, with the worst of the heat gone, Perugia was full of tourists. Shopkeepers tried to entice them with attractive shop-windows and popular music. I didn't pay attention to either, still racking my brain, worrying about the best solution for my mother. Suddenly I noticed a familiar tune coming out of a speaker in a small alley: a song by a black American blues singer and guitar player called Keb'Mo'. I had bought his CD during the 1998 North Sea Jazz Festival in The Hague. Never before had I heard Keb'Mo's songs on the radio or in a public place, only through my CD player at home, but there he was, unmistakable, and his words seemed intended especially for me. "Hand it over, give it up, give it over, get on your knees and pray."

I froze in my tracks, feeling goose bumps all over my body. Who had put on that song? Who was trying to convey a message to me? Slowly, I felt a strong conviction grow in my mind. I had to choose the Christian surgeon and then hand it all to God. I would still have to organize things, but I knew that I needed to let go of the worrying, because everything would be fine.

When I came home, I tried to tell Jan what happened in that alley without crying but, as I was searching for the right words, my eyes overflowed anyway. He just took me in his arms and prayed, thanking his Father for guidance and support.

As Jan had already told Cristina at the end of her last phone call about the house, it wasn't just "wait and see," but "pray, wait, and see."

CHAPTER TEN

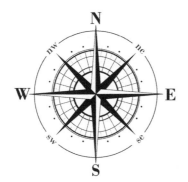

The Contract

I was lying on the queen bed in our one-room apartment. Jan had gone out to attend a prayer meeting at the church, and I had not wanted to join him. Actually, we had an argument about it. Jan thought that, after my experience in Perugia, I was ready to jump in head first, but I wasn't ready at all.

"But we're talking about your mother! You don't want to pray for your mother?" he said to me.

I felt uncomfortable hearing his thinly disguised reproach. Of course, I wanted the best for my mother, but how could I pray if I had still so many doubts about the Person to whom I was supposed to direct my prayers? Jan left alone, not understanding my hesitation.

At first, I felt sorry for myself, but then I thought I might as well try to find out more about that Person. I grabbed Peter's book, *Challenge to Encounter*. It approached basic questions, such as "How can we discern truth?", "Does God exist?", "Who is Jesus?", and "Is the Bible God's word?" It actually defied my convictions, beginning with a challenge to have an open mind about the value of Christianity.

As I read it, I discovered that my skepticism with Christianity was largely caused by a lack of knowledge. For example, I had never studied the Bible or its history and, yet, I was discarding it as a collection of myths, legends, and lies. I had assumed that, *if* Jesus had really lived, he surely hadn't been any more than a good teacher. Now, this little book was forcing me to take a stand, or at least to honestly consider the claims of Christianity. It stated that, eventually, the quest for truth leads us to a confrontation with Christ. I felt that this was true and, in consequence, I had a choice. I could keep running away from this confrontation, denying that such a thing or such a person could be real, and continuing my search for sense elsewhere, or I could enter the battle openly.

Right now, my mind was chewing on an intriguing citation that I just read:

> I am trying here to prevent anyone saying the really foolish thing that people often say about Him: I'm ready to accept Jesus as a great moral teacher, but I don't accept his claim to be God. That is the one

thing we must not say. A man who was merely a man and said the sort of things Jesus said would not be a great moral teacher. He would either be a lunatic – on the level with the man who says he is a poached egg – or else he would be the Devil of Hell. You must make your choice. Either this man was, and is, the Son of God, or else a madman or something worse. You can shut him up for a fool, you can spit at him and kill him as a demon or you can fall at his feet and call him Lord and God, but let us not come with any patronizing nonsense about his being a great human teacher. He has not left that open to us. He did not intend to.–C.S. Lewis, *Mere Christianity*

I looked for the flaw in the reasoning, but I couldn't find it. So I had to accept one of these opinions about Jesus as my own. Did I think Jesus was a psychopath, a demon, or God? The next chapter would explain more about the Bible and its reliability. Maybe, after reading that, I could still maintain that Jesus was a myth, just another character in a fairy tale.

As I pondered the problem, I flipped through the pages and saw that, in the back of the book, it said, "If you want, you can now decide to become a Christian." A model prayer showing how to do it was printed as well. I don't know what made me do it–maybe just a curious, *Let's try*–but I prayed to Jesus to come into my life, forgive me, and change me. I didn't feel anything. And I didn't tell Jan when he came back. I wasn't convinced that it had worked.

The next morning, Cristina called us with news from Dariella. Paolo had called her to know more about her meeting with Larry. She had told him that Larry hadn't made a better offer, but that she had given him several more days to reflect on it. Paolo then increased the pressure, telling her that we were about to give up on the house, and that she was pushing her luck, risking losing both potential buyers. She promised to think about it and call him back in the evening.

Immediately after Cristina's phone call, Jan prayed, blessing Dariella and Larry again. I realized that, after last night's prayer, I probably should have joined him, but embarrassment held me back. For some reason I didn't want Jan to know about my prayer. It was my private battle, a struggle with myself. Or was I fighting with God?

Very good news reached us that evening; Dariella had decided to sell the house to us and accept the offer we had made! However, to make it official, we had to put the whole thing on paper, to be signed by both parties. The next morning, we sat in the realtor's office to make the *proposta*. The atmosphere was one of excitement, but we were also a bit nervous, because Paolo and Cristina weren't sure whether they could trust Dariella after her meeting with the other Dutchman. Cristina created and printed the document. We signed it, and off it went, via fax, to Dariella in Rome. Our offer would be valid until midnight that same day. Would she sign it and fax it back in time? What if she called Larry, and he made a higher offer?

Back at home, Jan read his Bible, prayed, and continued blessing both people. We didn't talk much, just sat on the white plastic chairs under the elm tree. Time was hanging heavily around us. I tried to read one of the books Sandra had loaned me, but could not concentrate. It was hot. Cicada chirping mixed with frogs croaking. We had coffee. We had lunch. We had tea. The dogs were lying around lazily, not bothering to get up, not even to beg for a cookie.

Then, at 5 p.m., our cell phone rang. *"Pronto?"* It was Cristina! Yes, we were ready to hear the news… Cheering, Cristina told Jan that she had just taken the signed *proposta* out of the fax machine. The house was ours! We jumped out of our chairs and danced and shouted for joy! Finally we could take our plans off the shelf again—how to renovate the house, how to arrange the rooms, where to plant fruit trees, where to make the dog kennel, when to move in our furniture from France… all could now be reality! We couldn't stop brainstorming and, filled with excitement, we continued talking about our new place far into the night.

The next day we shared the good news with Vittorio and Gabriella, our landlords. They seemed relieved. Probably, they had asked themselves why we had done nothing but wait for a house that wasn't available. Alternatively, maybe they had been reluctant to give us notice to leave. At a wooden table outside a kitchen under the house, where Gabriella was working with her mother, we continued to talk about our new place with Vittorio, who nonchalantly smoked a long filter-tipped cigarette.

While chatting, we watched how the women filled small glass jars with a boiling sauce that came out of a type of food processor. Most likely, they had been working all day, because there were more than a hundred jars lined up on the table, along with stickers to be put on as soon the content had cooled. I was slightly puzzled as to why the eco-biological products they sold weren't manufactured in some sterile production environment, but the food processor aroused my curiosity. Raw, coarsely chopped ingredients went in, and a smooth, cooked sauce came out.

The *mamma* lit up when she noticed my interest and pointed out some details of the machine, which she lovingly called "Bimby." "Do you like cooking?" she asked.

"Oh yes I do, especially Italian food," I answered.

She seemed very pleased and offered to come to our apartment later that week to share some secrets of the Italian kitchen. I accepted eagerly. Having a real Italian *mamma* teach me cooking– what a privilege!

When she knocked on our door one afternoon, I was surprised to see that she carried a huge bag; she had brought her Bimby. She seemed determined to demonstrate all of its functions and asked me what possible ingredients I had available. I opened our tiny fridge and took out some vegetables. As a real chef, she gave me commands to clean this, cut that, and put it all in the machine. She was extremely talkative and didn't stop praising her food processor, explaining its ins and outs while we worked.

In went the ingredients; out came a lovely smelling pasta sauce. When I had emptied and washed the Bimby, she asked whether I had eggs, but I didn't. She called her daughter and commanded her to bring some. "There we go," she said satisfied, as she broke the eggs above the Bimby and added milk and a lot of sugar. She told me to put some cookies in a bowl and, a short time later, she poured steaming custard on top of them. A dessert was ready. The speed of her activities startled me. I washed the bowl of the Bimby again, and we repeated the procedure with other ingredients.

After two hours, our small table was loaded with saucers and plates, each filled with food. I'm not sure whether it was the Italian cooking I had expected, but I surely was impressed. As I began to thank her for her time and energy, she caught me off guard. With a sweep of her arm, she pulled a sheet of paper out of the big bag—an order form for the Bimby!

"Here I need your name and address, and here is where you can sign," she instructed me.

I was perplexed. Trying to swallow my disappointment and embarrassment, I asked, "Yeah, uhm… but… how much does it cost?"

"Only 1,200 dollars," she answered.

What? She must have seen the confusion on my face, because she began commending her Bimby all over again. I interrupted her, apologizing for not having realized that this was a sales demonstration and telling her politely that there was no way we could afford to spend that amount of money on a food processor. Probably, she didn't believe me because, with few words, she packed up her machine and briskly walked out. Later, I was relieved to discover that the painful incident hadn't changed the relationship with Gabriella and Vittorio.

During the last week of August, in the smoky office of a notary in Perugia, we lived the big moment. We signed the preliminary purchase contract for our house! We also learned that there were problems with the land registry; some type of survey hadn't been done. Cristina and Paolo informed us that it would take, at most, three weeks to sort that out. Depending on when I went to the Netherlands for my mother and my nephew, we could sign the definitive contract no later than mid-September.

We continued to plan and organize for the renovation and furnishing of the house, searching, shopping, and asking for references and prices. Of course, we didn't forget to go to the *Questura* to get our *permesso di soggiorno*. Unfortunately, the permits weren't ready yet, and the man at the counter couldn't tell us when they would be. After some pressure from our side, he scribbled a telephone number on a piece of paper, to call in a few weeks. We hoped that we could avoid standing in line for nothing yet another time.

Then Jan's nephew Paul phoned with the news that my mother was about to be called up for a pre-operation check-up and would probably be operated within two weeks. Worry crept in. Would it be possible to postpone the signing of the contract? However, before we could ask, Cristina called. The appointment for the house was delayed by three weeks, because another problem had been discovered. She assured us that it had been resolved; it only slowed down the whole thing. We didn't know the details and decided not to ask, because we trusted our realtors. Unfortunately, later we found out that they hadn't known the details either and had no idea how much delay there would actually be. Nevertheless, for now, I was able to go to the Netherlands without pressure.

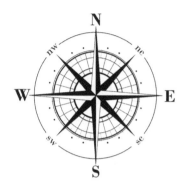

CHAPTER ELEVEN

The Deepening

The Netherlands, mid-September 2004

"Oh, look Mom, there he is!" We were watching through the window of my sister's house and saw her holding her son, who had been released from the hospital at the end of August, now two weeks ago. She saw us too and walked to the front door to let us in, still holding her baby. Dave was almost eight weeks old and gorgeous, but as tiny as a newborn; this made sense since he had been conceived about nine months ago.

When Elisabeth gave him to me to hold, at first I just stared at him, in awe. The miracle of new life. His dark eyes wandered, and his right hand clasped my little finger. "Hello there sweetie, I'm so happy to finally meet you. I'm your Auntie Milly. Cootchie, cootchie, coo!"

What is it with babies, why do they make me speak with a small voice and utter all sorts of funny noises? Elisabeth looked at me, a bit disconcerted. Babies don't do that with her. When she communicated her son's name to us, it came with the connotation that he was always to be called *Dave*, and never *Davie*. She was a brave, strong mother, and maybe it's exactly that what helped her through the difficult months after Dave's birth. However, I just gave in to my wimpy nature and continued playing the crazy aunt. Dave's eyes stopped wavering and now fixed on mine; he was probably fascinated by the ridiculous sounds I was producing. That moment I silently asked Jesus to bless him and protect him. I also prayed that, one day, I would have a child of my own.

Yes, I prayed. Although still not completely convinced about God's existence, I was continuing my spiritual battle and had now included prayer. In one of Sandra's books, I had read that man is made in the image of a triune God—who is relational in himself. Therefore, man is a relational being. The book also explained that we have an enemy, called Satan, and that he has a purpose: to disrupt any relationship, especially the one between man and God, in hopes of arriving at his ultimate scope, the destruction of humanity. According to the book, one of the weapons God has given to us is prayer, because when we put ourselves in a place where we have communion with God, the enemy loses ground in our hearts. So yes, I prayed. And I prayed a lot, because there was so much to pray about.

I had taken my mother to the hospital for the pre-surgery examination that morning. Everything was fine, and the operation had been scheduled for the next week. Earlier that week, at my mother's house, I had tried to collect all of the documents needed for the preliminary check-up. Since my father died more than a year ago, my mother's confusion had increased. She was still a zealous housewife, so her little rented row house was very tidy. The only problem was that she now put things away without remembering where she had stored them. While I was searching for her National Health Security card, I came across a small number of Watchtowers, the magazine of the Jehovah's Witnesses. "Mommy, look what I found, where did you get these?" I asked her carefully.

She answered a bit uncertainly, trained by my father never to buy anything at the door and never to let strangers in the house. "Uhm, there are these girls, and they are so nice. They speak about beautiful things, and we just chat a little bit."

When I kept on asking, she told me the whole story. Two women visited her at least once week and had taken her a few times to their meetings. My mother loved the company and the friendly words. I didn't know a lot about Jehovah's Witnesses, except for the money-driven, rigid organization that is behind them, but somehow I felt that this wasn't a good thing. I tried to explain it in simple words to my mother and told her that I was about to ask them not to come back. Although she said she understood, I saw the disappointment in her eyes, and I gave her a big hug.

That night, before going to bed, I prayed and asked God for wisdom. Almost immediately, a thought popped up in my mind.

Go and search for a Christian church in this city. Why hadn't I come up with that idea earlier? I switched on my father's computer that still stood there, unused, next to the spare bed where I slept. The computer connected to the Internet and, after I had typed the correct search arguments, I found the website for a church called "The Well." I wrote down the address and the time of next Sunday's service and felt peaceful about it.

Then I looked at a small pile of books on the bedside table. For the very first time in my life, I had visited a Christian bookshop, about a half-hour's drive from my mother's house, driving the car that I had rented to get her to and from the hospital in Amsterdam; she lived about 125 miles from the Dutch capital. I spent a couple of hours in the shop, trying to find the books that would answer the many questions I still carried within me. The title of one of the books I bought was *Jesus: Who is He?* by Tim LaHaye. After getting comfortable under the covers of my temporary sleeping place, I picked it up and began to read.

To come to a conclusion about the person of Jesus, the writer used the Bible to study what others had said about him, what he had said about himself, and what he had done. In the beginning, this made me rather skeptical, because I thought it was circular reasoning. Something like, "using the Bible to prove the Bible is true." "Internal evidence," LaHaye called it. Anyway, as I read along I learned a lot, not only about Jesus, but also about the Bible.

It amazed me how the writers of the Old Testament books had already predicted so many details of Christ's person and life, centuries before he was even born. It fascinated me to read about how unconventional Jesus had been to expose the rigidity of the religious leaders who had ignored the heart of God's commandments, while he had come to reveal it. It intrigued me that he had told Satan nobody should be worshiped but God, and yet Jesus allowed people to worship himself. The internal evidence said that Jesus not only believed in God, he knew him personally. He was the invisible God made visible. He had come to live and to die as a human being, to enable people to be reconciled with him out of love, compassion, and the desire to have communion with them. And the best thing was his resurrection, which must be true; who of his disciples would have been willing to undergo persecution, torture, and a cruel death for a lie? They were sure he was risen from the dead and they knew he was alive. Did I?

The Sunday morning my mother and I went to the church I had found on the Internet, we arrived at a large building that had once been a school. To create more space for the meetings, they had added an annex in the form of a semicircle. Actually, it turned out to be the first time they had used the building in its new form, and the service both celebrated God and inaugurated the new building. It was a joyful meeting with beautiful songs—yes, I shed some tears—and a short but sincere sermon by a gentle, young pastor. After the service, everybody went outside to release colorful balloons, all of which had pieces of paper with Bible verses attached to them. My mother enjoyed the festive atmosphere, and she smiled as we watched the balloons ascend in the bright blue sky, higher and higher, until an air current caught them and carried them slowly out of sight.

Back inside the church, we followed the smell of coffee to the café, where round tables with small sugar pots, milk cans, and baskets with cookies stood waiting for us. I made my mother sit down and went to the counter to get us a cup of coffee. While waiting for my turn, one of the women I stood next to asked me, in a friendly tone, "Good morning, I haven't seen you before. Are you here for the first time?"

"Well, yes I am, but actually I'm here for my mother," I answered, and I told her about living in Italy, my father's death, my mother's loneliness, the Jehovah's Witnesses, and my search for an alternative.

She was exactly the right person to talk to, because she assured me that it would be no problem to fetch my mother on Sundays and bring her back home. In addition, she would make sure that someone would visit my mother at least once each week. Wow, I hadn't expected so much kindness right away. I also told her about my mother's operation. She replied, "Call me as soon she's recovered and wants to come to church," handing me her telephone number.

When I returned to my mother, I found her chatting away with some people who had come to sit at her table. She looked at ease, basking in the friendliness that surrounded her. Between sips of coffee, I asked the person next to me where they lived. She explained that they were from the center of the country and here today because of an NCMI meeting. To show interest I asked, "NCMI? What is it, and what does the abbreviation stand for?"

She looked a bit sheepishly when she answered, "I know it's a network of churches, but to be honest, I don't know what the acronym means. I'm sorry."

I didn't mind. After all, I was here for my mother, not for myself, and I had already achieved my goal for the morning. However, when we walked to the exit of the church, I saw a rack containing a solitary flyer, right next to the door. Its title was "NCMI– Who Are These Guys?" Following a flicker of curiosity, with my mother clinging to one arm, I reached out with the other and put the flyer in my bag to read later.

CHAPTER TWELVE

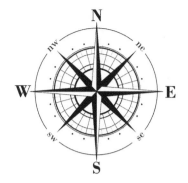

The Operation

R iding a bicycle along the Amstel River, I was on my way to Amsterdam. The friends with whom I was staying during my mother's time in the hospital lived about ten miles away. I had returned the rental car, because I wouldn't need it in Amsterdam and, besides, riding my friend's bike was so much better! Although highways and airplanes slightly polluted the view—the Amsterdam airport was close—I enjoyed the typical Dutch landscape that surrounded me: the low horizon where endless blue skies, holding billowing white clouds, met green fields feeding black-and-white cows, and the meandering river mirroring it all. Oh, that river. If there was one thing I really missed doing since we left the Netherlands, it was gliding over the Amstel River in a slim line boat with my rowing mates. It was good rowing weather; a slight breeze barely rippled the surface of the water, leaving no waves in its midst.

As I watched the water, the picture suddenly struck me. Until now, my life had been shallow, as if I had missed out on something. Not that my pains and disappointments hadn't stirred up the waters and rocked the boat, but I longed to live life fully, profoundly, instead of just skimming its surface. *Wait, didn't Jesus say something about having life abundantly?*

While pondering this thought, I noticed a boat rounding a bend and coming my way. A men's eight. The cox steered around two swans that swam majestically across the river. I heard his voice giving steady, staccato commands, accompanied by the rowers' rhythmic sliding and the simultaneously splashing oars… my existential considerations gave way to myriads of memories. How many times had I rowed on this water? I allowed my mind to drift away to scenes and emotions of the past as I pedaled my bike towards the city that appeared in front of me.

Gradually, with the buildings and traffic increasing around me, my thoughts returned to the present. Today my mother would have her operation. In fact, the surgery had already begun. Jan's nephew Paul had told me that I could come to the hospital and wait, while he attended the surgery and would give me a report every now and then.

I had taken Mom to the hospital the day before. Everything had been okay, and she was rather relaxed. The only thing that had upset her was the fact that she had to wash her hair. "I washed it yesterday!" Styling her hair was one of her weekly rituals. She washed it, applied her lotion, carefully curled her hair around her rollers, and then waited until it was dry before removing the rollers. Subsequently, a special combing method (and many hairpins) assured her of the hairstyle she had always had, never changing for as long as I could remember. Had she now carried out the whole procedure for nothing? I explained to her that she must wash her hair with the special disinfecting shampoo the nurse had given her to prepare for the surgery. Grumbling and muttering, she gave in.

When I had left her that evening, her grey hair wet and limp against her small head, my heart hurt. She looked so fragile. Would she be up to the major surgery? And if her body could cope, would her mind be up to the challenge, or would the anesthesia pull her into even deeper confusion? So I had prayed again.

I arrived at the hospital, a large building in the east of the city, and I parked the bike, putting two huge chain locks on it: one to fix the front wheel to the frame and another to attach the whole bike to a piece of immovable urban furniture. Unfortunately, in Amsterdam bicycles are an attractive item for thieves. I entered the hospital and installed myself on one of the plastic chairs in the spacious, modern visitor's hall. The architect had done everything possible to create a lighthearted atmosphere, installing huge windows, immensely high ceilings, and tiled floors. The area looked more like a square in a modern district than a hospital entrance. I sat across from the open reception counter, where friendly, casually dressed women seemed ready to answer any question.

When Paul came to update me on the progress of the surgery, he didn't seem to notice that the bloodstains on his white gown and plastic clogs clashed horribly with the intention of the architect to achieve a carefree environment. I didn't dare to ask whether it was my mother's blood, but instead tried to focus on what he told me about the surgery and the surgeon. His eyes sparkled as he explained how this particular doctor expressed his amazement at God's design of the human body during every operation. I wondered what the man thought about why the failing bodies needed his surgeries, but I didn't ask. Paul explained that my mother's heart needed a new cardiac valve and four bypasses, and the necessary arteries for the bypasses were being taken from her left arm.

The operation went well and took about six hours. My brother, who worked close to Amsterdam, joined me in the afternoon. We were allowed to see Mom at the end of the afternoon after she had regained consciousness in the recovery room. When we finally stood at her bedside between machines, drips, and white curtains, and softly called her name, she opened her eyes and greeted us with a smile. First, she recognized Nick and then me. It was if somebody opened a faucet from above and filled my veins with pure joy! The overflowing delight didn't come only from knowing the operation had been successful, and my mother was well, but also from the growing confidence that God existed, or put in a better way: that he was alive and heard my prayers. Of course, I didn't share this with Nick.

My mother was to remain in the hospital for ten days and, afterwards, she wouldn't go immediately back to her little house.

Instead, she would be taken care for in a special home in her city. During every day of her hospitalization, I rode my bike along the Amstel River into Amsterdam and back again, and each time I saw her improve. The pain became less and less intense, and she regained her mobility, thanks to a patient physiotherapist.

Finally, the moment arrived when I had to book a flight back to Jan in Italy. I had been in the Netherlands for almost three weeks, and he told me he missed me. Of course, I had missed him as well, but I also understood that I had had a lot of distraction, so to speak, while he had merely been waiting for me to come back. I longed to return to Italy, but it felt as if I was failing my family by leaving on the very day that my mother would be released from the hospital. A bit like a project leader quitting the project before it was finished. My brother assured me that he would take care of her, and we both assured our sister that she was not to worry about visiting Mom every weekend, since she now had a small boy who required her care.

As the airplane descended into Rome Airport, I noticed how yellow the land was. It had seldom rained in the past four months. After landing, I stepped out of the plane into hot, dry air. Although I already missed the Dutch green landscape, I knew I was back in the country where I belonged.

CHAPTER THIRTEEN

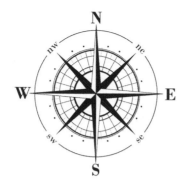

The Move

Mid-October 2004

T he weather was still warm and, because of some thunderstorms, the air was humid. I slapped a mosquito from my leg as we watched the surveyors move their instruments. We had just arrived at the property that was supposed to be ours soon, and now we were waiting for a potential supplier of floor tiles. Dariella, the owner, had told us that we could enter the house whenever we needed to prepare for the move. Seeing the surveyors at work, we realized that the land registry procedure hadn't been concluded yet.

"*Buon giorno!*" we greeted them.

They looked up, disturbed.

"May I ask you something?" I continued, trying to get past the men's obvious irritation.

With a sigh, they acknowledged the interruption and stopped their attempts to put their equipment solidly on the uneven ground. "*Si?*" answered the oldest while he did his best to put on a friendly face.

"Well, it's just that we would like to know when the land registry procedure will be finished, because the realtors told us that we could sign the definitive purchase contract for this house any day now."

He scowled, as if I had insulted him severely. "Forget it," he said. "This will take at least six weeks."

What? A quick calculation made it clear that we wouldn't be able to move in before December. Disappointment mixed with indignation. Why hadn't anyone let us know that we would have to wait at least another month and a half? We wanted to live and work here, create a place of our own, instead of lodging in the one-room apartment at Vittorio and Gabriella's. The still-comfortable temperatures would drop within a few weeks, and the apartment had no heating. Furthermore, we had begun to feel useless. By now, we had almost finished interviewing potential building material suppliers to prepare for the work at the house and were just waiting for some quotes. We called Cristina to tell her what we had heard from the surveyors and asked for an explanation. She was as surprised as we were and promised to find out more as soon as possible.

When she called that afternoon, prospects had changed completely. Dariella had proposed that we sign a *comodato d'uso*, a mutual agreement that allowed us to use the house without payment, the commencing date being a week later. We accepted the proposal. We couldn't begin the renovation yet, but at least we would have a place for ourselves!

The next day, after we had signed the agreement at the realtor's office, Dariella called us. She was friendly and said that her brother and son were coming to the house to collect some personal items, and then told us that we could have everything else in the house. In addition, if there were problems, we could always call her or her father who had previously begun the house's renovation, along with his late son-in-law.

After the phone call, we returned to Poggio to make a list of the items we would need to buy. The house was full of furniture, most of it worn, if not broken, all of it filthy and downright ugly. However, apart from the table and the chairs we had already used when we had met Dariella and her family in August, we found some armchairs and a small table we could use. In addition, there was a cupboard full of pots, pans, plates, cups, glasses, and cutlery. The rusty, moldy fridge on the balcony seemed to work, and there was a greasy twin-burner attached to a gas cylinder that was at least half-full. In one of the three small, smelly bathrooms, we spotted a water heater. One of the four bedrooms contained a frame for a double bed, a clean mattress, and a wardrobe that didn't fall apart. We also found an old telephone. According to Dariella, the telephone subscription was still valid, so plugging in the telephone should connect us to the network. Okay, we would have to do some serious cleaning but, overall, we were positive. We would manage until our own furniture arrived from France.

We couldn't begin working on the house, but Paolo had made clear that we had better get to know the procedures we would need to follow to ask for permission for the renovations. "This is Italy," he said with a smile, but his tone was slightly sarcastic. He put us in touch with an architect and, together, we came up with the idea that since we couldn't work on the house, our first project would be the land. The architect introduced us to Fabio, a farmer who also worked as a day laborer for others. As soon as Fabio looked over the land that would be ours, overgrown with brambles, broom, and briar, he decided that Forest Service needed to be involved before he could begin the clean-up. A Forest Service employee, who happened to be in the neighborhood, came the same day. He told us that we needed to hire an agricultural engineer to study the land, write a report and submit the request. It began to dawn on us what Paolo had meant by "this is Italy."

On the day that the agreement to use the house started, we moved the first load of our belongings from our apartment near Perugia to the house in Poggio. With a sense of victory and ceremony, we opened the front door, but these emotions quickly subsided when we discovered that the fridge, twin-burner, gas cylinder, and water heater apparently had been considered personal items. They were all gone. Even the old telephone wasn't there anymore.

Jan blessed Dariella once more, and we decided not to let this minor setback ruin our day. Furthermore, we had a bigger problem to deal with; the next day–six months since our emigration from France–the French car insurance would expire, and the Italian insurance agency refused to take the car until it had an Italian license plate. To be able to request one, we needed the technical data sheet for our car, to be sent by the Italian Land Rover importer, but we hadn't received it yet. Without a car (and for how long?), it would be difficult to live in our new home, being three miles from the nearest shops. A phone call from Brad from the Perugia church, with whom we had shared our problem, brought a solution. A friend of his, Giovanni, had a small car he couldn't afford to insure, but he was willing to loan it to us. We drove to Giovanni's house to arrange for the car and insured it for three months, hoping that we would be driving our own car long before the end of the insurance, so that Giovanni would be able to benefit from it too.

Meanwhile, we had got our residence permits from the *Questura*. Although we were expecting to stand in line for a long time again, a friendly police officer picked us out of the queue, asking us whether we were *extracomunitari*, that is, whether we came from a country outside the European Communion. When we told him we were from the Netherlands, a member of the European Communion, he pointed us to another office window that had no line at all. We wondered whether this was a new procedure, or that during our previous visits to the *Questura* nobody had bothered to point us to the right window. We were happy to receive, finally, our permits, but when we turned around from the European citizen window and saw the colorful, multi-ethnic line of people waiting patiently for the only other window, we felt a spark of guilt. Were we facing an attempt at efficiency or just blatant discrimination?

After having spent the very last night in our temporary apartment, we packed the remainder of our things and moved to Poggio. On the way, we bought a two-burner, a telephone, and a powerful portable grass trimmer. We might not be allowed to bring in bulldozers yet, but we could no longer sit still and do nothing. Once we arrived at the house, we unloaded the car and did our first serious cleaning job to get one bedroom and one bathroom ready for use. A couple of hours later, we sat satisfied in the midst of old furniture, our own belongings heaped around in random piles. To celebrate, we opened a bottle of wine and toasted to our new house, while eating an improvised dinner consisting of crackers and cheese. A luxurious diner in the most expensive restaurant couldn't have made us happier. We were at home, finally! The next day, for one last time, I would return to the apartment where we had spent our past five months, to clean it and to accompany the horse transport to Poggio. Oh, by the way, after we plugged in our new telephone, we discovered that the line was dead.

A couple of days later, we went to visit our nearest neighbors, whose house was situated about 300 yards down the steep road. We brought them a box filled with products from our French campsite, which the friendly, white-bearded man—his name was

Luciano—accepted, pleasantly surprised. He had just returned from work; his wife Valeria wasn't at home yet. We chatted a bit about who we were and where we came from, and he explained that the property we were about to buy had once belonged to his family, but he had sold it years ago to build a new house on a piece of adjacent land that he still owned. Therefore, he knew a lot of the property's history, something that would turn out to be convenient for us.

To make up for the loss of some of Dariella's things, we bought a fridge and a water heater. The fridge was delivered and installed by the friendly shopkeeper. Jan installed the water heater himself, and I relished the prospect of a good hot shower to wash the dust and dirt out of my hair. However, the hot water didn't reach the shower, and the kitchen tap and the other bathrooms didn't seem to be connected at all to the water heater. In addition, the flush suites of the toilets didn't fill up, so we had resorted to the "bucket method." Jan concluded that the water pipes were clogged up, and we spent an afternoon pouring acid in tubes to soak off and dissolve the lime, which came out as a yellowish, muddy substance. The water, coming from a well next to the house, obviously had high calcium content! Our work had only partial results; we could stop using buckets, but the shower was still miserly with its water flow, as if the water pressure wasn't high enough. We had to dance around under the drizzle to get wet all over, but at least it was warm.

We called Dariella about the dead telephone line and the water problem. She promised to call Telecom, the Italian telephone company, and referred us to her father for the water problem. When we spoke to him, he advised us to check the level in the water tank, which was located on a slope about 50 feet above the house. We had guessed as much that the water from the well, before reaching our taps, was pumped into that tank, so that the difference in altitude could give the water a natural pressure. We hadn't thought of checking the water level though; we had just switched on the pump a few times.

We walked up the path leading to the tank, working our way through the plants that had been growing, undisturbed, for almost three years. The tank was an enormous, old iron cask on its side, measuring at least 2,500 gallons, the manhole facing heaven, and its short legs pointing helplessly in our direction. Jan climbed the small ladder that stood against one of the legs, turned around, and put one foot on the tank. He removed a big stone that held the manhole cover in place, opened the hole, and popped his head in. "I don't see anything," he said. His voice sounded hollow from within the tank.

"Maybe because there isn't anything," I replied, standing at the foot of the ladder. "It sounds rather empty."

Jan shifted his feet, trying to bend his body into a more comfortable position, and dug in deeper. "Wait, I see something now," Jan said as his eyes got used to the dark. "And I have bad news."

The tank was drained, almost to the bottom. At least we now understood the cause of our water problem; there wasn't any.

When we had met Dariella and her family in August, her father had assured us that water would be available all year round. We now turned to our neighbor Luciano to find out the truth. He said that maybe we hadn't understood.

"If you fill up the tank while the well has water, you might manage to have water all year round. But if the tank is empty now, you have a problem, because during summer the groundwater level normally drops under the level of the pump and it has hardly rained, so the groundwater hasn't risen again."

"What about the water pipes we've seen next to the house. Shouldn't these be connected to the water mains?" Jan asked.

Luciano began to laugh, but he didn't sound happy at all. "The water mains? They asked us years ago to put in the water pipes and promised to connect us to the mains, but nothing ever happened. This is Italy, you know. You'd better get used to the Italian ways!"

Our neighbor sounded bitter, almost ashamed about the state of affairs in his own country. We refused to absorb his bitterness, but because this was the second time in a few days we heard a native belittle Italy, we began to prepare our hearts for many long procedures.

That evening Jan prayed, "Lord, you have brought us to this house. We trust that we will have water enough for ourselves and our animals."

CHAPTER FOURTEEN

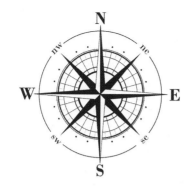

The Advance

First week of November 2004

I couldn't believe what was happening here. We sat in a
restaurant, having dinner with Anna and Claudio. Instead of
having a peaceful evening, enjoying one another's company and
sharing experiences, we were listening to how the two people at
the other side of the table bickered and quarreled. It was not only
that they were ruining our evening together; I was particularly
disappointed because my expectations of Anna had been high.

We had met Anna in church. She was Dutch too and an amiable,
radiant personality. Until this evening, I had hardly spoken
with her, but Jan had gotten to know her better. As a former
teacher, Anna now taught Bible lessons. During my weeks in the
Netherlands, Jan had started to take these lessons to prepare for

his baptism, which would take place in December. Anna and her husband Claudio, a non-Christian Italian, had lived many years in the Netherlands, but Claudio had a dream to run an *agriturismo* in Umbria, so they had moved to Italy two years ago. The move had been much against Anna's will, but she had followed her spouse. She, together with their three children, now lived in a small hamlet with some rickety houses that, together, formed the future *agriturismo*, in the only building that wasn't under construction. Claudio spent most of the time in the Netherlands for his work, because creating the *agriturismo* was extremely costly.

Jan had told me that Anna was filled with the Holy Spirit and that she spoke in tongues. I was skeptical and a bit jealous at the same time but, above all, I was curious. I had read about spirit-filled people, but I had never spent time with one in person. She would surely be very spiritual, infallible, and a source of divine wisdom, right? Wrong. She was just like me, just another human being with human weaknesses. Later, Anna became a good friend of ours, but that evening I felt so disillusioned!

Needless to say, I was still struggling with God. Some days I thought, *Yes! I'm sure he's real!* On other days—such as this evening—I wasn't convinced at all and wondered whether he wasn't just one big fake, with so-called believers all happily participating in the collective deceit. A Santa Claus for adults. I *wanted* him to be real, I *tried* to believe, but it was as if something in my head jammed on the brakes every time my heart quickened at the idea that Jesus was right there with me. However, in spite of my reservations, I continued going to church.

For several reasons, Jan felt that Brad and Sandra's church wasn't the place where God wanted us to stay. Along with some other people, one of them being Anna, we made the step to a smaller group. The about thirty people in this other community were warm and seemed genuinely interested in us. The first Sunday morning we attended, a visiting pastor conducted the service and, during the worship, encouraged us all to seek God's presence. I watched amazed as many people wept and Jan slid almost off his chair.

To me, God was still far away and I didn't experience any supernatural presence at all. I knew, though, that something was missing in my faith. I had prayed that Jesus come into my life, and I wanted to believe, but I didn't talk about it. I didn't declare out loud, "Jesus is Lord," as the Bible told me to. I just couldn't say it. Was it pride, lack of faith, or fear of being a fake? I didn't know, but I continued my wrestling match.

At home, we still had no telephone, little water, and no car insurance. We also had no news whatsoever from the realtors about the land registry and no date to sign the purchase contract. Day temperatures had dropped from around seventy to under fifty degrees. The nights were so cold that we slept in our sleeping bags under the blankets. The fireplace, in which we burned dead wood found around the house, produced more smoke than warmth. After two days of being well smoked, we bought a wood stove to put in the fireplace. This stove gave more heat, and its stovepipes took the smoke, through the chimney, out of the house. At the local lumberjack, we ordered a cord of wood chopped to the right size.

Concerning the Italian license plate that we needed to insure our car, we thought we had gathered all necessary documents to request it. However, the local office of the *Automobile Club d'Italia* (ACI) informed us that we needed a certified translation of the French vehicle registration certificate, as well as a residence statement, that is, the registration with the town council of the address where we lived. The resolute woman in the ACI office said that I could do the translation myself and then get it certified at the courthouse in Orvieto. With all of the complicated Italian procedures we had going on, this one seemed too easy. In fact, when I went to the courthouse it turned out that I couldn't get my translation certified, because my name was on the car's registration certificate as well. But Jan's name wasn't, so he could go back another day to try to get the certification.

The same ACI lady told us that we could go to the town hall of Poggio to ask for the residence statement, and they would print it for us right away. Well, this wasn't that easy either, because the local police officer had to verify that the house was fit for habitation and confirm that we really lived in it. He promised to drop by the day after to do the residence verification.

The next day, no officer, no wood. We did have a lot of water though, coming from a grey and threatening sky. The clay soil, which had become *terra cotta* during the hot summer weather, changed in no time into a six-inch deep swamp of thick mud. The horses made their way with difficulty through the muddy soup in the small pasture that we had managed to fence off between the bushes. Most of the hay for the horses that we had bought from Fabio was trampled into the ground before it was eaten.

At first, we tried to keep on working outside, because it was so motivating to clear the area around the house. We had discovered low, natural stone walls and uncovered young olive trees and fruit trees—apple, pear, fig, and medlar—from a thick blanket of brambles. However, it was raining too much and the ground was too muddy, so we gave up. The good news was that the ground water was rising. After all, Jan had prayed for water, hadn't he?

At the end of the day, the lumberjack called to tell us that he would bring the wood next morning around 9 a.m. When he still hadn't shown up at a quarter past ten, we left for Orvieto to get the translation of the vehicle registration certified. We really needed our Land Rover back, especially in this weather, with a dirt road that extended for two miles. This time everything went smoothly at the courthouse, and Jan got the required certified translation. Check! With most of our wardrobe still waiting in a French storage facility—and two suitcases of summer clothes—we also bought some warm sweaters.

When we arrived back at home, the first thing we noticed was a huge pile of wood logs in front of the house, in the pouring rain. So much for dry wood. The second thing was a note from the police officer stuck on our front door to let us know that he had visited. Well, at least he could have looked through the window and seen that the house was fit for habitation; it was furnished and we had left the lights on. In addition, while he was at the door, the three dogs surely would have livened things up a bit, as we hadn't wanted to leave the poor animals outside in the rain.

We stepped into the corridor and immediately got alarmed.

"What's that stench?" Jan asked me, sniffing around.

"Oh no, look there! How embarrassing!" I exclaimed, being the first to enter the living room.

On the tiled floor were the three dogs, guilty looks on their faces, and one big dog doo, clearly visible from the outside. Of course. I chuckled while cleaning up the mess, and hoped that the officer, now he had verified that the house was fit for habitation, wouldn't doubt our qualification to inhabit it.

Later that day, in between rain showers, we loaded two wheelbarrows and carried more than 4,000 pounds of wood to a dry place under the house. Afterwards, we sat tired but satisfied in front of the burning wood stove, talking about our renovation plans. We had already noticed that the living room was dark, but with winter approaching and days shortening, we now had to keep the lights switched on all day. The house had the shape of a reversed L, and the living room was situated in the L's internal angle, facing west. In addition, the roof of the porch leading to the front door was screening off sunlight. The south side of the house—the reversed L's foot—had all the light and the view over the valley, with Orvieto in the distance. Three bedrooms, side by side, occupied that part of the house. We decided to change our plans drastically and open the walls between the bedrooms to connect them and make a big living area. The original, dark living room would become a study and, hopefully, at some future time, a bedroom for a little one.

While we were chatting away about our new plans, someone knocked on the door. The dogs began barking like crazy, and we looked up, startled. Our first visitor! It was Luciano, our neighbor, carrying a bottle in each hand: one with homemade olive oil and another with home-distilled *grappa*. To welcome us to our new place and (probably) to reciprocate our gifts. We were pleasantly surprised and invited him in.

"*Tutto a posto?*" he asked, checking whether everything was okay.

We explained about the purchase of the house and the problems with the land registry. To our astonishment, Luciano turned out to be involved as well. A relatively small part of the land we were about to buy was *his* property, not Dariella's. Luciano had given it to Dariella's husband to use, but it still belonged to him. However, the preliminary contract stated that Dariella was planning to sell it to us, so she had a problem. We began to understand why it was taking so long to sign the definitive contract; it wasn't only the land registry.

In spite of all the adversities, we never doubted that the house would become ours. We were sure that we were in the place we were supposed to be and felt confident that it would all work out. In fact, after I had called Telecom for the fifth time, a *tecnico* showed up and replaced more than eighty feet of telephone cable that had been eaten away by mice. At last, we had a working telephone!

It continued to rain, and although our neighbor had complained about it because he had to postpone his olive harvesting—he owned about 400 neatly maintained olive trees—we were grateful for the water. The rising groundwater was pumped into the tank, and the water pressure gradually improved. The bathroom drizzle was slowly changing into a real shower. The agricultural engineer came to inspect the land and told us that she didn't expect that we would have any problems getting the permit to clear it (although it would probably be months before it arrived). And we got our *residenza*! Check! With the residence statement and the previously obtained certified translation of the vehicle registration, we immediately set forth for the ACI to complete our request for an Italian license plate.

We felt so confident that we even called the French moving firm to transport our furniture to Italy at the end of November. The only potential problem we saw was that the huge truck with an attached trailer would not be able to drive down the last, very steep and narrow part of the road leading to our house.

During the night before our furniture was to arrive, I woke up and lay with my eyes wide open, staring into the darkness of the cold bedroom. We were sure the movers wouldn't make it to the house. Last week Jan had contacted Fabio, the farmer who was going to clear our fields, to ask whether we could rent his *camioncino*, a small pick-up truck. He had promised to let us know whether his truck would be available, but we hadn't heard anything yet. Although we had tried to call him on his mobile several times, he hadn't answered the phone. What would the French movers do tomorrow? Unload their truck and trailer and leave our 2,000 cubic feet of furniture on top of the hill half a mile from our house? In the silence of the night, I prayed a short prayer, "God, thank you for providing a solution for the problem with the big truck." Peace flooded my mind and I fell asleep again.

At 7:30 in the morning, the telephone woke us up. It was Fabio! He had noticed the lost calls, but hadn't recognized the number because we had called with the landline that finally worked. Something had prompted him to take the phone book and look up the number. When he found out the address of the phone number, although still in Dariella's name, he realized who called him and remembered that he had forgotten to let us know about his pick-up truck. He exhausted himself in apologies and offered to bring the car right away. Half an hour later, it stood in front of the house.

In the meantime, the movers called, desperate. They were in Poggio but afraid to take a wrong turn, so they wouldn't go any further until someone came to guide them to our house. We wondered about the small-town-mindedness of these international movers, until they told us later that, very early that morning, they had lost their way and had found themselves in the center of Orvieto. I had done that once with the Land Rover and I had nearly panicked. The narrow streets and alleys of the city on the butte of volcanic tuff were designed to be walked on, or at most ridden on by horse and carriage, not driven by vehicles over a hundred horsepower strong, let alone by massive trucks with trailers.

After the coffee, we started working. Afraid that they would find themselves in trouble on the dirt road with the loaded truck and the trailer, the movers had left the trailer in a parking lot in Poggio. They indeed parked the truck on the hill half a mile from our house and were happy with Fabio's pick-up, which they drove back and forth between their truck and our house countless times. It took us the whole day to unload the truck and carry everything inside. Most of it went into the empty house, the part where we wouldn't live. The slender Frenchmen managed to carry even a heavy couch and heavy cupboards inside, almost running up a dilapidated staircase that led to the entrance.

The next morning they brought the trailer and, another half a day later, we had emptied that as well. The movers left for their homeland, relieved that they had finished their job in the middle of nowhere or, as they described it, "at the end of the world." We too were thankful that the move had worked out, that we could replace the rickety, ragged furniture with our own, that we could sleep in our own bed, on our own mattress, under our own comforter, that we had even found the remote control of the television (in the very last carton we had opened, of course).

When Fabio came later that day to get his *camioncino* back, I marveled at how this friendly man, who hardly knew us, had followed a divine prompting so that God could provide his solution. Seeing God at work, answering my prayer, allowed my faith to grow another tiny bit.

CHAPTER FIFTEEN

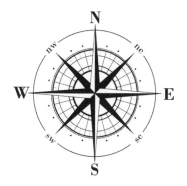

The Surrender

A cold Sunday morning
in December 2004

We entered the church room, which was located under an apartment building in Perugia, and saw three enormous pans, each on a huge single burner. It was the equipment that Italians use in August, when they sterilize dozens of jars of homemade *passata di pomodoro*—tomato sauce. This yearly preservation procedure assures them of good pasta sauce until the next harvest. Obviously, it was neither the season nor the place to can tomatoes. The pans contained plain water that was being heated for the baptismal pool. Today was the day of Jan's baptism, a happening he had been looking forward to for a long time.

While we were still in France, he once told me that he wanted to be baptized, but that it would probably change him. I had felt awkward and afraid. Would I lose my husband? Now the baptism was at hand, I had grown enough to know that if the water did change him, it would be for the better. The basic Bible study with Anna had prepared him well, so he understood the meaning of baptism. "The outer testimony of an inner decision to follow Jesus Christ," he had explained to me. However, he expected more of the event than having it just be a formal, albeit important, confirmation of his commitment to God. He desired to receive an anointing fire of the Holy Spirit, so that he could start to work and be useful for him. He had been praying and fasting the last week, just for that.

Jan's first fast had been difficult for me. With so many people on earth dying from starvation, I was convinced that having food available was a privilege. Why would God require us to abstain from eating? Furthermore, from what I had read about him, I was sure he wouldn't want us to fast as a kind of sacrifice to use in negotiations to get something from him in return. First, the Bible stated clearly that Jesus had made the sacrifice once and for all, and we were not to add anything to that, as if his work at the cross wasn't enough. Second, if God was open to bargaining, he wouldn't be sovereign (and I wouldn't like him). Later, I learned that God loves it when people hunger and thirst for more of him.

One day, Jan returned from a prayer walk—a new term in our vocabulary—and exclaimed, all beaming, "I think I've spoken in tongues!" He had been at the small stream at the border of our grounds, down in the valley, and had prayed fervently to be able to speak in unknown languages. When he opened his mouth, out came incomprehensible sentences. I must admit that I doubted the authenticity of his "tongues." Sometimes I had tried it as well, and it wasn't too difficult to fake. But, then again, would my husband really cheat about something that was so important to him? Was my intellectual pride hindering my heart from accepting things too wonderful to understand?

Happy for Jan, but still fighting for my own faith, I sat among the people in the church who listened to his concise but clear testimony. Of course, it wasn't new to me, but I enjoyed hearing again how Jan, born in a Christian family, was about twelve years old when he had a dream that somebody knocked on the door of his room. When he opened the door, he saw a man standing before him. His parents had explained that it was a special dream, in which Jesus had asked Jan to open his heart and let him into his life. At about the same age, he had prayed that he would dedicate the last 25% of his working life to God and, afterwards, had calculated that it would start at the age of fifty-five. He was honest about backsliding as a teenager and later as an adult, about his repeated repentance, and thankful for God's endless grace and mercy. He shared how, in spite of his many mistakes, he had felt led and supported by Jesus during his business career, especially during his job as the managing director of a national distribution firm. He explained how his faith had deepened while living in France, and how it had led to his baptism, which he saw as the beginning of a new "career" as a servant of God.

Finally—the burners had needed a long time to let the temperature of the water rise a few degrees—he stepped into the 2 x 7 foot portable PVC baptismal pool, filled with lukewarm water. Anna, his Bible teacher, kneeled down next to the pool and baptized my husband in the name of the Father, the Son, and the Holy Spirit. When he rose from the water, his face grimacing with emotion, he raised his arms in a gesture that reflected both exultation and worship. As he slipped into the white bathrobe I held before him, I kissed his lips to congratulate him and noticed mine getting wet with the water that had buried my old husband, so that the new one could rise and walk in a new life, as Anna had explained before baptizing him. There wasn't much time to ponder over these words, because I had to sing.

Along with some other people, I had practiced three songs to celebrate Jan's step and, although I still wasn't a professing believer, I loved to participate in the music. In France, I had taken singing lessons and had sung during the music evenings we had organized on the campsite. Now I sang in church. It would be the first of many times.

My favorite song of the day was "More Than a Friend" by Jeremy Riddle, and it was the last of the three songs we performed:

> In the quiet of my soul
> In the stillness I hear your voice call
>
> . . .
>
> Jesus you're more than a friend
> Jesus you're more than my heart could ever express

What twist of mind was enabling me to sing these words with all my heart and still maintain that I wasn't sure whether I believed? Whatever it was, it was about to be adjusted. No sooner had we played the last notes of this beautiful melody than I saw a short man standing before me. I recognized Mario, who had preached the first time I had visited this church in October. We had never talked before, but he looked me straight in the eye and said, "I have a word from God for you."

The message took me by surprise, and I just stared back at him.

He continued, "God says that you have to quit fighting and stop seeking, because you already believe."

Then he turned, pointing toward the small baptismal, and said, "Obedience is not in reading books; it is in the water."

Awe and confusion filled my being. How was this possible? How could he know? Then it dawned at me: Mario hadn't known, but God had. God had just spoken to me through a man. He had said that my little faith was enough for him. I doubted him, but he didn't doubt me. He didn't judge me, he just encouraged me to take the last step: declare publicly that Jesus was my Lord. He loved me and wanted me to be his.

While I thanked Mario for his words, I couldn't hold back my tears when the full realization of what just happened washed over me. I went back to my chair, overwhelmed, and wept silently.

After a while, people around me also sat down, and Jan, dried and changed, prayed over the Lord's Supper that was about to be taken. During the few months we had attended, I had always refused to take it, because it was clear that only real believers should. This time, it was different. Although I hadn't verbally professed my belief that Jesus was my Lord, I was about to make a public statement. When the communion tray passed before me, I took one of the small cups of wine and a morsel of unleavened bread. I felt looked at and ill at ease while I chewed and drank. Had I made a mistake by partaking? Having swallowed the bread and the wine, I looked desperately around me and found Anna and Mario close by. They were watching me, as if they were waiting for me to say something. I asked them to pray for me. As they did, I felt the awkwardness leave me and make room for a sense that everything was all right. I had come home. Finally, I had given up struggling. I had surrendered.

Afterwards, driving back to Poggio, a shining Jan confessed that two years before he had prayed that God would lead us to a place where we both could be baptized. It seemed we had reached that place!

The next three months I devoured the Bible studies that Jan had done previously with Anna. My hunger to get to know God better and to grow was enormous. I didn't change overnight though. The modeling process was slow and sometimes humbling; I not only got insight into God's character, but also into mine. Often, before I knew it, I caught myself getting irritated again, giving a heated reaction, or having a half-hearted attitude towards Jan.

God also made me look at my past through different eyes. I had always considered myself a good person and a victim of bad deeds and circumstances but, from my new, painful, perspective, I recognized how my striving for personal happiness, brought about by my godless world view, had made me an extremely egocentric person. He didn't justify the sins committed against me, but simply showed that I had been sinning too. For example, in my relationships, I had always been expecting the other person to love me unconditionally, and whenever I doubted that type of love, I emotionally checked out until the relationship broke up.

Looking back, I also recognized how God had called me more than once in my life, even during periods of sin and utter selfishness. The most obvious time had been ten years ago, when I was in the middle of a wrong relationship. I attended the funeral of my 95-year-old grandmother. Her death didn't affect me, because we had never been close and, unfortunately, her dementia had taken her even further away. The ceremony consisted of an unemotional Protestant sermon in a sterile room of a funeral parlor. While the family members, including me, sat through the service with deadpan expressions, at one point the minister gave the sign to sing Psalm 23. Reluctantly, people began to sing, struggling with the slow pace and the dull melody, "The Lord's my Shepherd, I'll not want; He makes me down to lie in pastures green…"

Suddenly, completely unexpectedly, something seemed to snap inside me. From the very core of my being, an intense sorrow welled up, and my unstoppable sobs broke the surface with incredible force. While I cried uncontrollably, my mind frantically wondered what in the world was happening to me. After a couple of minutes, the emotions ebbed away, and I succeeded in regaining my composure, highly embarrassed, as I had been the only person showing any emotion.

Now, looking back at that situation, I understood that it hadn't been my own emotions emerging out of nowhere. In some supernatural way, God had allowed me to look into his heart to feel the profoundness of his love and his grief for me in the midst of my ungodly life. He had told me that I was not to depend on man's love to find happiness; he was my Shepherd, only he could restore my soul, leading me to the green pastures I would never find in this physical world. I didn't hear him. Still, he never gave up on me and, patiently, lovingly, kept pursuing me.

Thinking about this and other moments of my life, I was so thankful for his eternal love and his forgiveness. In my capacity as a newborn child of God, adopted into his family, he had granted me the possibility of being transformed into the image of himself, my Father, the One who had created me in the first place. Gradually, it became less difficult to swallow my pride, admit my mistakes, and apologize without the urge to excuse my misbehavior. I learned to rely on him for healing my heart, and he helped me to forgive the people who had hurt me.

My baptism was planned for March 2005, three months after Jan's. But first God taught us another lesson.

CHAPTER SIXTEEN

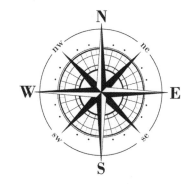

The Baptism

February 2005

Someone knocked on the door of the house that we could finally call our own. The week before, we had signed the purchase contract. It had been a cheerful and relaxed event with eight participants: the realtors Paolo and Cristina, our neighbor Luciano, the owner Dariella and her brother, the notary and us. When everything was signed and settled, to everyone's surprise, Jan opened a bottle of Prosecco and filled champagne flutes for all to share and celebrate.

I walked to the front door of our house to see who had knocked. A young couple stood on the porch, curiously watching me.

"*Buona sera*," I greeted them in Italian, but the man replied in English, "Are you the new owner of this house?"

From his accent, I recognized immediately that he was a compatriot and answered in Dutch. The man turned out to be Larry, our competitor in the race for the house, who Jan had blessed at least a thousand times. The young woman was his wife. I invited them in, feeling sure of our victory. The house was ours now. Jan, sitting at the computer, didn't know who they were when we entered the living room.

"Jan, this is Larry, the man who wanted to buy this house as well, with his wife," I introduced them.

Jan raised his eyebrows in amazement and stood up to greet them. "Hello, nice to meet you! What brings you here?"

Larry explained that they were passing through Umbria on their way to Sabina, a hilly region in Lazio, north of Rome, where they had bought a plot to build a house. "I was just curious to discover who had bought the house in Poggio that I've been interested in, so I decided to come and look!"

When Jan asked why they hadn't carried through on their purchase attempts, Larry continued to explain, "Um, well, I'm a real estate developer. Normally, when I set my mind on a property, I get it, no matter what. And in the beginning, I really wanted this house, because it has many possibilities. However, after the last talk to Dariella in August, I somehow lost my interest, I don't know why. That's when we decided to look in Sabina, a region we both love. There we found a beautiful site, which we ended up buying. We're now on our way to talk with an architect to prepare for the building project."

Jan and I looked at each other, knowing who had made Larry lose his interest in our house.

After half an hour, Larry and his wife continued their trip and left us utterly astonished, praising God. Not only for granting us the house, but also for talking to us through this situation. He had just said to us, "You see? I told you to bless your enemy and you were obedient. Now I wanted to let you know that you have prayed in my will, and that I have answered your prayers. That's why I sent Larry." God had shown us the power of blessing.

Larry had found us in the house in its original state. Although it had been ours now for over a week, we weren't allowed to start our renovations, because the *tecnico* of Poggio hadn't yet approved the project. On the other hand, the approval to clear the fields had been secured. Fabio worked a full week with a huge bulldozer to clear the site of its growth. After that, a colleague of his worked two days to sow hundreds of pounds of grass seed. Then Fabio loaned Jan his *cingolino*, a small caterpillar tractor, to turn over the surface of the soil, so that hungry birds wouldn't devour the seed. Because this work left us without pastures for at least two months, Luciano allowed us to put the horses in his olive grove. We had noticed the electric wires around vineyards in the region and had also spotted many prints left by wild boars on our now barren grounds, so we fenced off a small piece of land that Jan had plowed for a vegetable garden.

Meanwhile, I had finished the basic Bible study with Anna. Jan and I had initiated her next course, called "Radical Disciples," together, and it was encouraging to be able to share. The first "sermon" I prepared in the context of a practical Word administration exercise was about God's covenant, his agreement that he was to be our God, and we were to be his people, in a loving, faithful relationship. Suddenly I saw the coherence between the Old and New Testament, how God's salvation plan through his incarnation in Jesus Christ is the thread throughout the entire Bible. I loved Augustine's way of expressing it, "The New [Testament] is hidden in the Old and the Old is fulfilled in the New." I grasped how God's grace in Jesus Christ distinguished the new from the old covenant, enabling us to be his children through the indwelling of the Holy Spirit upon our repenting and believing the gospel. I learned that the Greek word for testament could also be translated "covenant," implying that the whole Bible is about God's covenant with humanity.

I thrived on studying God's Word! Not only did it reveal a loving God who desires to save all people; for the first time in my life, I began to understand the larger story of the human race and the make-up of human beings, something to which my psychology study, with its countless and often contradictory theories and problem solving methodologies, never had contributed. What I read in this collection of sixty-six books, written by forty different people over the course of fifteen centuries, made sense. It explained what made the world tick, what made men tick. Only information that is true can explain reality in such a complete way, and I realized that the Bible contains truth, absolute truth, inspired by God himself. Just like the author of Psalm 119, I rejoiced at God's word, "like one who finds great spoil." It became very precious to me.

After we completed Anna's disciple course, we didn't feel that we had finished learning. We wanted more. It was then that the NMCI came into view again. I was sure that it hadn't been a coincidence that I had met people from the NCMI network six months earlier, when I was in the Netherlands for my mother's heart surgery–or that I had found the last NCMI flyer in the church rack next to the exit. We learned that *NCMI* stands for "New Covenant Ministries International," and when we looked up their website, we found out that they were a non-denominational group of people with a vision of a New Testament pattern for discipling the nations and equipping believers to do exactly that. Their approach and Biblical foundation appealed to us. They had their beginnings in South Africa and proposed a curriculum of distance education in collaboration with the South African Theology Seminary. We decided to start our studies with them after my baptism.

That Sunday morning in March, there were no big pans with water on huge burners. Instead, the pastor and his wife had brought jerry cans of hot water from their home to add to the cold water that came out of the church tap. When the PVC baptismal pool contained enough water to submerge me, and I had changed into a long white dress of heavy cotton, I started sharing my story with the gathering.

My testimony was long. The fact that I talked in English, while somebody else translated my words into Italian, further doubled its duration. As I spoke, I realized that the smaller children became annoyed and even began to play with the baptismal water—and were corrected by their parents. Other people, such as Sandra, the American missionary, and a dear friend who had come over from the Netherlands, listened closely. A part of me got a bit embarrassed that I took so much time, but the biggest part wanted to tell every aspect of my struggle to give glory to the loving, living God, who had never given up on a stubborn, proud woman. I described to the congregation how I had been raised and how I had lived: as an atheist, always trying to be in command of my own life, convinced that I was a good person, and that my capacities would get me the happiness I was looking for. I explained to them that I had studied psychology because I wanted to understand the essence of human beings, and that I never succeeded. I spoke of how I had always been in search of unconditional love, but had been disappointed and hurt—and had hurt other people—along the way. In addition, I told how I had tried to seek purpose in life through my ever-increasing work responsibilities, to no avail. Last, I shared with them how I had persisted in thinking that only weak and stupid people needed to invent themselves a god and a book with life principles, because they either couldn't or wouldn't take responsibility for their own lives. "As you may understand, God has had a tough job to change me to what I am today."

I told how I had tried to escape from God, denying, doubting, and fighting him, and how he relentlessly pursued me, during almost thirty years, to touch my heart with his love and grace.

"Now I don't doubt or fight anymore. I still have questions, but I know that's not a problem for God. Although I discovered that there is more to me than my brains, he doesn't want me to act brainless. He created me with the capacity to search and to do research. If and when he wants, he will give me the wisdom or disclose the knowledge to find the answers. I am at peace. What I used to describe as irrational, I now recognize as spiritual. It's not only that I believe that he exists, it's much more: I experience his presence within me as I feel his love, and he fills me with pure joy. I am so thankful that Jesus never stopped calling me, and that I have found him, the revelation of the living God, who has a plan for all of us, also for me, better and more fulfilling than I can ever imagine. I have finally found perfect love. In spite of everything I have done wrong and still do, Jesus loves me forever, and God forgives me time after time. He taught me that, in my pride and rationality, I was the one who was weak and foolish. I see now that being strong without God is fake strength. I fought him so long, but it was only when I surrendered that I won in power, because that was the moment his Spirit came to live inside of me with *his* strength. Only now am I wise, with a wisdom that begins with faith in God. Thank you God, thank you Jesus. I want to follow you, whatever it takes."

When I finally finished my testimony, the pastor invited me to step into the small pool. The water had gotten cold, and I shivered as I slipped, waist-deep, into the water. But, inside, anticipation warmed me. I had learned that baptism was more than the public display of a decision to follow Jesus, more an act of obedience. If Jesus commanded every believer to be baptized, it had to be more than a ritual, because he explicitly disapproved of empty tradition. Having studied what the apostle Paul had written in his letter to the Romans, I was convinced that something in my spiritual being would change.

Then the pastor spoke the long-awaited words, "I baptize you in the name of the Father, the Son, and the Holy Spirit." He pushed me under, lifted me up again, and as I got up, dripping, I felt joyful, refreshed and very much alive. In my immersion, I had identified with the death and burial of Jesus, my Savior, and so declared the old, selfish, always-wanting-to-be-in-control Milly dead. Rising from the water, I was resurrected with the living Christ and, clothed with my new identity in him, was ready to start a new life in a covenant of love with God.

Afterwards, Jan shared with the people in church that God had given him the text of Isaiah, chapter 12, as a personal word for me, explaining that God would use me to make his deeds known among the people. Of course, I also sang after my own baptism, and although the lyrics weren't precisely written for someone who only recently converted, I had chosen "The Heart of Worship" by Matt Redman, because I realized that worship isn't about singing a song.

I'll bring you more than a song
For a song in itself
Is not what you have required
You search much deeper within

My prayer was to become a worshiper and to be able to use my musical skills, for what they were worth, to enter into a deeper communion with the Holy Spirit living in me and to bring other people along.

That spring we started working on the house. Many evenings we found ourselves on a chair, with NCMI study books on our laps, in the midst of the chaos and dust we had created during the day. We loved embellishing the place where we lived, working towards the design that had finally been approved by the authorities. Still, we thought it was even more beautiful to work on ourselves. I longed to change into the image of my Savior and to drink always from his thirst-quenching presence.

Much to my confusion and frustration, I entered a desert instead.

CHAPTER SEVENTEEN

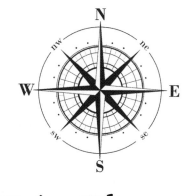

The Desert

May 2005

We were at the office of the *Servizio Idrico*, the Water Board Company. Our neighbor had said that it would be impossible to connect the house to the water mains, but we had decided to request the connection anyway. We knew that, for God, everything was possible. When we had filled out the necessary forms, the man in charge told us that we would have water within three days. In front of him, we were able to conceal our perplexity but, outside the building, we looked at each other rather astonished. Then I said with a big smile, "Does he realize that this is Italy?"

"Now, where's your faith?" Jan replied, laughing as well.

It didn't take exactly three days, but before the hot Italian summer began, we were connected—and our neighbors as well!

The water pipes were filled, but my womb was still empty. Since our arrival in Italy one year ago, I had carried out at least seven pregnancy tests, because my periods seemed to have become irregular since we were trying to have a baby. Each time the result was negative, and my heart hurting. I went to a doctor to have my hormone levels tested. The result was difficult to digest: menopause was setting in. I was only forty-three. Would God's plan for our lives exclude a child?

In the period after my baptism, I felt myself slip out of the oasis of joy and gratitude and gradually wander off into an area run dry with dejection and listlessness. I didn't want to go there, but I was unable to stop myself. Anger and irritation consumed me. At the same time, I felt criticized and judged. I didn't understand what was happening. Was it because I would never carry a baby? Were old emotional wounds that cried out for healing luring me into the wilderness? Did bitterness or pride clot the umbilical cord that connected me to the fountain of God's love? Or was it all simply the result of hormonal changes?

I felt so tired, so lonely. I prayed to God. I begged to understand, so that I could do something about it. Once, I thought God was saying to me through Psalm 147 that I had to sing for him to get out of the blues, "Praise the LORD! For it is good to sing praises to our God; for it is pleasant, and a song of praise is fitting... He heals the brokenhearted and binds up their wounds." But

I found it difficult to sing when feeling down. Instead, I was looking inside of me, soul searching, digging for possible causes of my depression. We had discovered Christian satellite TV and watched many programs. I was so thirsty for a solution to my problem that I clung to the words of television preachers, waiting for the magical formula that would bring water to my desert. I tried out every piece of advice, prayed every prayer for deliverance, and attempted to chase away every evil spirit. I made a list of all people I might need to forgive and I asked forgiveness for all possible sins I had committed in the past and for those which I might still be guilty of in the present. I read my Bible daily and declared every verse that spoke about love, peace, and joy in my life. At the end, I still felt barren, weary, and useless. And at fault. Maybe that was the worst feeling; I was to blame for not being a joyful, grateful, tenderhearted Christian. I knew God was with me, but I didn't sense him. I knew Jan loved me, but I didn't feel it. I was well aware that, at times, I was unbearable. While Jan was busy serving and developing his spiritual gifts–praying for healing and encouraging people– in the Perugia church, I was struggling with myself and was often downright blunt and bitchy. Jan tried to understand me and he said he loved me anyway, but it wasn't always easy. The more interior turmoil I experienced, the more I shut down, making it all the more difficult for Jan to reach out to me. At times, we had arguments about the lack of affection I displayed towards him, making me feel like an even greater failure.

One Sunday morning in December of 2005, I was particularly down. Half an hour before we were to go to church, we ended up reproaching one another, using hurtful words. As always when we fought, I burst out crying in frustration and, in no time, my eyes were red and my head was throbbing.

"You go to church alone! I won't go with you!" I growled at Jan.

"Very well!" he snapped back.

He put on his jacket, took his Bible, and went outside without further speaking to me. I heard him walk down the stairs, start the Land Rover, and drive away, leaving me by myself in a heavy silence. As I was drowning in self-pity and feeling utterly lonely, my silent sobbing quickly changed into loud crying.

"Jesus, please help me, pleeeaaase!"

Although I didn't feel the slightest sliver of divine presence, I just knew that he was my only hope to get out of the wilderness. Tired of introspection, I reached out to him. I told him that I trusted him for restoration, for healing of whatever was wounded inside of me, and for reconciliation and harmony in our marriage. I repented of all the bitterness and anger that I harbored. I prayed that Jan would forgive me, and that we would be able to talk in love and pray together.

While still weeping, I sang:

> I trust in you, my God
> You are my shield
> You gently lift up my heart

While you're saying that
You won't leave me
You will give me strength
My hand is in yours
I won't worry
If you are with me
I will fly with wings of an eagle.

I repeated the song over and over again, my voice unsteady with tears. I didn't feel any change. It was as if the words bounced off the ceiling. Nevertheless I continued, like a stubborn child. If I didn't want to be buried by the blinding sandstorm of my emotions, I had to continue and seek the shelter of his presence. "The LORD is near to those who have a broken heart, and saves such as have a contrite spirit." I needed to have faith.

When Jan came back in the afternoon, there wasn't a miraculous improvement, but we were at least able to talk. It was emotional as we cried and prayed together. I asked both Jan's and God's forgiveness. I realized now that digging and delving inside my head and heart would never change me; I had tried that all my life. Only Jesus could transform me, that is, if I let him. I handed it over. As David had cried out to God in Psalm 139, I prayed, "Search me, O God, and know my heart! Try me and know my thoughts! And see if there be any grievous way in me, and lead me in the way everlasting!"

I didn't understand how it worked, but I also let go of the urge to reason out everything. I knew this though: it was by the power of surrender that I could succeed. A couple of months before I had heard a beautiful song called "On My Knees," sung by Jaci Velasquez, but it was only now that I grasped its full meaning.

> I get on my knees, I get on my knees;
> There I am before the love that changes me.
> See I don't know how, but there's power
> When I'm on my knees.

I had tried to hear from God in the way that Jan often did: asking for and receiving the numbers of Bible verses. In our immaturity, we had even done a test, assuming that the Holy Spirit would want to communicate with both of us at the same time. We prayed and asked for a Bible verse simultaneously, then shared what we had received. Of course, the verses I had "received" were different from Jan's verses. Mine didn't have a clear message or didn't even exist, and it was obvious that my relationship with God wasn't as good as Jan's was. I had felt frustrated and inferior, but also rebellious. Now I understood that the Holy Spirit communicated in various ways. There wasn't a better or worse way. God had spoken to me through a song, and although it wasn't the first time he had done so, I hadn't recognized his voice.

A few weeks later, at the beginning of 2006, Jan asked me to join him in a three-day fast. In the course of my first year as a Christian, I had accepted that fasting was a way of praying and not a sacrifice as I had thought before. So I agreed—we would abstain from food to add force to our prayers for deliverance from our past, anointing for our ministry, and direction for the future. It was my first fast, and it was a horrible experience! I had little energy to pray. I tried to read my Bible, to hear God's voice, to feel his presence, but I only felt either hungry or sick. Doubts about the use of fasting crept in again.

Then, at the end of the third day, while I sat dizzy, dull, and desperate with the Bible on my lap, God spoke to me through the book of Psalms. First, I felt strongly led to Psalm 32, which talks about the joy of God's forgiveness, but also speaks of his promise to guide us if we submit to him. "I will instruct you and teach you in the way you should go; I will counsel you with my eye upon you."

Then he brought me to Psalm 78, a lesson about how the people of Israel kept wandering around in the desert after God had led them out of Egypt, complaining and rebelling in spite of their deliverance and God's provision. "How often they rebelled against Him in the wilderness, and grieved Him in the desert!" "Yet he, being compassionate, atoned for their iniquity, and did not destroy them; he restrained his anger often, and did not stir up all his wrath. He remembered that they were but flesh, a wind that passes and comes not again."

God had led Israel into the desert on their way to the Promised Land. But why? To test their faith and faithfulness, to see if they were worthy of their destination? I meditated on this possibility, but in the end, I didn't think that was the case. God didn't bring Israel in the desert to be tested; the journey through the desert was a natural section of the route to the Promised Land.

A journey in God's presence! In the past they had called out to him, and now there they were; he had heard them, set them free, and was guiding them to the land of milk and honey. Were they grateful? Well, they had been immediately after their deliverance from the Egyptian pharaoh, who they had seen disappear under the water of the Red Sea, along with his army. The people had even sung together, "The LORD is my strength and song, and He has become my salvation; this is my God, and I will praise Him."

However, shortly after, they fell back into their old habits of grumbling and complaining, reverting to old idols, and feeling lost and miserable. God was present, saw it happen, confronted them and they didn't repent. There, in the wilderness, they went astray. Instead of confiding in God who, furthermore, was visibly with them and provided for them day and night, they looked at their physical circumstances and began doubting him and his promises. As a result, they kept wandering in the desert and never arrived at the next phase of God's plan for them. Not because they weren't worthy of it, but because they simply would not have been able to enter the promised land and face the challenges awaiting them there without totally depending on him.

Just as God had liberated his people from Egyptian slavery, so he had set me free from the slavery of sin and self. Now here I was, on my way to my spiritual destination. My past had disappeared under the baptismal water, and I had rejoiced in my new freedom and in my God, Jesus Christ. Sure enough, my physical and psychological circumstances weren't perfect. How had I reacted?

Instead of continuing to confide in God's presence, with his Holy Spirit living inside of me and gently guiding me, I had gone back to old ways of reasoning and wounds of the past; this continued to result in negative emotions. The Holy Spirit was illuminating the dark corners of bitterness and pride within me, because they formed stumbling blocks that prevented me from walking into my future.

God loved me too much to let me trip over my self-created obstacles, and he wanted to remove every single one of them. Nevertheless, he wouldn't do it if I didn't trust him. He wouldn't do it without my permission. I realized that God was telling me that I needed to grow in my dependence on him, and I was even able to thank him for the difficult period in the wilderness. It was necessary to demolish strongholds of wrong thinking patterns and to teach me to trust in him only.

Finally, he led me to Psalm 63. Suddenly I realized that he not only knew what I was going through, he understood my feelings! It had been God himself who had inspired David to write this psalm, to express these emotions. He was compassionate, literally. He felt my pain and my desperation while I was wandering through my spiritual desert.

> My soul thirsts for you;
> my flesh faints for you,
> as in a dry and weary land where there is no water.

And the best part was that his Word included the solution: turning to him, believing in his power and his Love, praising his name.

> So I have looked upon you in the sanctuary,
> beholding your power and glory.
> Because your steadfast love is better than life,
> my lips will praise you.

Then I read this verse, which would become one of my all-time favorites, "My soul clings to you; your right hand upholds me." I understood that I had to surrender completely and let go of the idea that I had to control my life, resolve every problem I encountered, and answer every question. He was the only Solution, the only Answer.

So here were the possibilities: continue my walk in the wilderness, in that lifeless no man's land where I allowed bondages of my past to form obstacles to total freedom, and thus my future, or submit to God and follow him in faith towards my promised land. I decided to cling to him.

Slowly but surely, something within me changed as I drank from his presence. Not that I would never again taste spiritual dryness but, a few weeks later, I was able to declare with all my heart from Psalm 108,

> My heart is steadfast, O God!
> I will sing and make melody with all my being!
> Awake, O harp and lyre!

I will awake the dawn!

     I will give thanks to you, O LORD, among the
peoples;

I will sing praises to you among the nations.

     For your steadfast love is great above the heavens;
your faithfulness reaches to the clouds.

Much later God would give me the image of a fruitful bush
in fertile ground, saying, "You will carry fruit, thanks to well-
digested painful experiences, which will serve as fertilizer for
your growth and make the fruit of better quality and more
numerous." The fruit would be the people who would get to
know God's love because of my testimony. I also knew that I had
to stay close to Jesus, the source of living water and perfect love,
if I didn't want to wither again.

CHAPTER EIGHTEEN

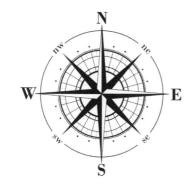

The Longing

February 12, 2006

I t was Jan's birthday, and we were on our way to Rome in a minibus with a Brazilian family. Thiago and Luiza were the pastors of a small church in the Italian capital, but they lived, with their four children, in a town about twenty minutes drive from our home. We had been happy meeting them because, until then, the nearest Christians we knew were in Perugia, more than an hour away. Thiago had invited us to visit their church, and we would have gone the week before if they had not forgotten about it. Not finding them at home and not knowing where the church was, we had gone back to Poggio. This Sunday, however, everything turned out well. In fact, we could not have planned it better ourselves; it was Jan's fifty-fifth birthday, the first day of the period he had promised to God, more than forty-two years ago, in which he would be available to serve him fulltime. God was keeping Jan to his promise.

A month later, we left the church in Perugia that we had attended for more than a year. We had loved the informal atmosphere of the small congregation. We were baptized there, had participated in Bible studies, and contributed to worship on special occasions. Jan had prayed with people and encouraged people. There was a lot of room for initiative. However, we felt that we had reached the limits of our growth there and that it was God's timing for a next step. Therefore, when Thiago and Luiza asked us to join them and serve in their church, which consisted of 70% Brazilian people, we decided to go to Rome every Sunday. We were aware, though, that it would be temporary. From our NCMI studies, we understood that the Biblical pattern is to have local churches, and two hours traveling time did not fit that definition. Thiago suggested that we move to Rome to assume an "official" role in the church. They themselves were planning to move as well. We explained to him what we thought was our part: helping him to establish structure and growth, not being part of the structure. After all, God wouldn't have led us to Umbria if he had wanted us to serve him long-term in Rome.

However, God used the period we were with Thiago and Luiza's congregation. We learned to serve him in the practicalities—participating in the worship, ministering to people with problems, helping to prepare people for a ministry, assisting with the organization of a spiritual retreat, and even conducting biblical leadership training for which we used what we had learned in our studies. But, moreover, he taught us about our own shortcomings. Coming from the north of Europe, we found it often difficult to handle our pastors' easy-going Latin American mindset. Although we loved them, we exchanged some harsh words in moments where our cultures clashed.

One afternoon, at home, Jan and I were talking through a difficult situation that had emerged recently and we used condemning words to express the frustration we experienced. Suddenly I saw Jan freeze in the middle of a sentence. Astonished, he looked at me and said, "God just spoke to me."

He hesitated a moment and swallowed before continuing. "I heard him say, 'If you handle disagreements with disrespect and bitterness, how do you expect me to give you more responsibilities?'"

Then he added, amazed, "I really heard him, with an audible voice."

We sat still, rebuked and ashamed, and realized how terrible our thoughts and words had been. If we were called to love, forgive, and bless even our enemies, how could we allow ourselves to nourish feelings of resentment towards people we called our friends? We bowed our heads, repented, called Thiago and asked him to forgive us for our bad behavior.

It was also during this period that God revealed details about how I could serve him. Now that I was approaching the boundary of my desert, he wanted to prepare me for my spiritual destination. In the early spring, a friend of Thiago's from Brazil, who came to visit Italy for a couple of weeks, prophesied that I would write words that would touch many people's hearts. Not much later, a Spanish pastor spoke a prophetic word to the whole congregation that stirred my heart and let my tears stream. It was a verse from Psalm 113, "He gives the barren woman a home, making her the joyous mother of children. Praise the LORD!"

Although the pastor had talked about spiritual children, born into God's family because of the Good News we would share with them, I felt God telling me that I would become a real mother of a real child. It confused me because, in the meantime, I had reached complete menopause. It hurt, but I had accepted his will for my life and tried hard to see the advantage of remaining childless; I would have more time to serve him. Still, the pastor's word touched me deeply and left me wondering about God's plans.

Late spring something changed inside of me. I noticed a longing to love and care for a child, no matter in whose womb it had been conceived. I had considered adoption before, but had discarded the idea, afraid that it would be too difficult. Now it was as if Someone had planted a seed in my heart, and this seed began germinating. Patiently, I let the sprout of this new desire grow and waited until I was sure it was strong and viable.

In August, I could no longer hide it and shared it with Jan. As with my original desire for a child, two years earlier, his reaction was positive. We talked about the possibilities, the waiting time, our own age, and the possible problems. We prayed together and agreed that we would start the procedure, confident that if it were really God's will, everything would work out so well that even we would be amazed. And, if it wasn't his will, he would bring it to a halt. Honestly, I didn't doubt that God wanted this to happen. I had received his word and had felt the desire come to life inside of me. Furthermore, didn't Psalm 68 say that he is the Father of the fatherless, who settles the solitary in a home?

Both my family and Jan's sons were in favor of our decision. Jan had one special request though: let it be a girl. Having raised two great boys during his previous marriage, he wanted this to be a new experience for both of us. I also loved the idea of having a girl. In fact, as a teenager I had already written letters in my diary to my future daughter.

In September, we went to the *Tribunale per i Minorenni*, the juvenile court in Perugia, to offer our availability as adoptive parents. It was the start of a long series of information sessions and interviews.

In the meantime, we had continued our studies and the work on the house. On the first floor, we had finished the living room, the kitchen, the corridor, and the terrace. In addition, because we felt that one of the things God wanted us to do was open the house for people who needed a restoration period, we had created a guest room with a small bathroom downstairs. Several people had already been blessed staying with us, feeling encouraged and refreshed.

We had also spent time on the creation of a website called *Italia per Gesù*, a portal to churches that wanted to increase the Kingdom in unity and collaboration, instead of sticking inside their own denomination—all of Italy united for Jesus. Later we understood that, although it was absolutely God's vision, it hadn't been God's timing, because no other church ever participated. We had to learn not to walk ahead of God.

In October, we heard through the grapevine that South Africans from the NCMI network were to visit Tuscany to encourage and teach church leaders. Although we were not official leaders, we longed to meet the people with whom we felt related through our studies. Therefore, at the end of that month, we took the train to Pontedera to meet Marcus and Adele. There was an immediate rapport. Not only did we like them as people, but the way they taught and encouraged made a profound impression. They were humble, lively, loving, and full of Biblical wisdom.

The main subject we discussed that afternoon was how to recognize, train, and release church leaders. One of the statements was that the success of a church depends on how its leaders behave *outside* church meetings. We were looking in a mirror, watching how we had developed and behaved in the past year, not always acting humble and loving. However, Marcus' teaching also revealed that we weren't really learning to be leaders. Although we had tried to implement the knowledge acquired during our NCMI studies in our activities within the Brazilian church, we had mainly leaned on our worldly skills and experiences, without being coached to do otherwise.

At the end of the meeting, Marcus and Adele prayed for us and shared an encouraging personal word with us: the role models for our current ministry were Aquila and Priscilla, the couple that Paul mentioned a few times in his letters. In the train back home, we had plenty to talk about and, in the end, one question stuck out. Had we finished another track God had put us on to prepare for something else?

During the days immediately after the meeting, we devoured everything we could find on the Internet about Aquila and Priscilla in an attempt to find direction for our ministry. We saw how many things we had felt and done, seemingly unrelated, came together. For example, we felt it was important to open our house to host fellow Christians and we were motivated to help other churches start, grow, and gain structure. We wanted to help the people to grow spiritually and to help train leaders, even to the point that we became restless when we saw that our help was no longer needed. In addition, we longed for unity in the body of Christ to let the Kingdom of God grow, instead of focusing on denominations.

We prayed a lot but, in the end, we agreed to stay in the Brazilian church, because we didn't feel God telling us to leave. However, we decided not take any more initiatives, because we wanted to be sure that it was God guiding us in what we did and how we did it.

On a beautiful November day, we picked olives from the misshapen trees on our grounds. It was the first time. In an attempt to restore the trees, Jan had pruned them drastically, and probably they needed more time to get back in form, because the harvest was small. Most Italians harvest their olives by stripping the olives off the branches, letting them fall on enormous nets spread out under the trees, drawing in the nets, and putting the olives in plastic crates. We, having no nets and few olives, handpicked every single olive and enjoyed the peaceful monotony of the repetitive movements on that quiet fall day. The autumn sun gave a golden glow to the bronze-green trees and a warm touch to the crisp air. Every now and then, we had to chase away the horses, whose curiosity brought them to investigate the contents of the crates.

Obviously, the hundred pounds we harvested weren't sufficient for the olive press to process in a separate batch. Luciano, having picked at least tenfold—with nets—suggested we join him, so next day we found ourselves in a noisy, intense smelling building, where the oil would be extracted. We hadn't expected to find a donkey turning millstones, nor the huge machinery we were now facing.

While waiting our turn, Luciano explained the process. The crates were emptied onto a conveyor belt that led the olives to the first part of the machine. Here, they were cleaned of stems, twigs, and leaves before they were washed in a water bath. Next, they went to the grinder, which crushed them into a paste that was slightly heated to increase the yield of oil. After about half an hour, the paste went into a centrifuge that separated the oil from the watery part. At the end of the machinery, a trickle of the greenest extra virgin olive oil flowed out of a small pipe into a metal container.

Luciano interrupted the trickle for a few seconds as he filled a small pitcher and beckoned us to follow him into a side room. There we found a burning fireplace, where slices of the traditional Umbrian salt-free bread were toasted to make *bruschetta*. Luciano introduced us to the best way to try out the new oil. He rubbed the toast lightly with a garlic clove, poured on an abundant quantity of the liquid treasure, and sprinkled a little bit of salt on it. With the first bite, my taste buds seemed to wake up and waltz with pure delight. I closed my eyes while I sensed the fruity fragrance of fresh-cut grass mixed with the creamy essence of almond. The flavor had nothing to do with any olive oil I had ever tasted before. Jan and I were more than enthusiastic and complimented the oil brought forth by "our" Umbrian hills.

Meanwhile, our joint batch had begun its milling course. To take our share of oil home, we had brought a few big bottles. Jan had also taken a small bottle he wanted to fill with the very first oil drops that would come from the machinery: our first fruits, which he wanted to use as anointing oil when praying for the sick. He would never make use of it, because later he understood that we didn't need to perform any ritual for God to heal. However, at that moment, God saw Jan's grateful heart towards the Lord of the harvest and he probably smiled.

Yes, we were grateful, both of us, and not just for our first seven liters of *olio extra vergine di oliva*. We had seen God at work in our lives and in our marriage. I knew that without his grace, without Jesus Christ transforming us, our relationship would have been very difficult. It even might have ended, as others had before, with me emotionally checking out because my requirements, my expectations about what I thought love was, weren't being fulfilled.

The difference between a marriage with Christ and one without him was immense. Without Jesus, I tended to look at my partner as either the source of my happiness, or the cause of my misery. With Christ present, I had learned to look at, listen to, and learn from him. He taught me to receive the grace to change from expecting to being served, to desiring to serve. With the changing prospect of my role in our marriage, I also realized that it didn't make sense to judge Jan's weaknesses from the point of view of my strengths. Nor did I have to feel inferior when I compared my failings with Jan's good qualities. God had united us to make us stronger together than each of us was apart. We were complementary. He had given us both a completely new view of love, beautifully described in the first letter to the Corinthians:

> Love is patient and kind; love does not envy or boast;
> it is not arrogant or rude.
> It does not insist on its own way; it is not irritable or
> resentful; it does not rejoice at wrongdoing,
> but rejoices with the truth.
> Love bears all things, believes all things, hopes all
> things, endures all things.
> Love never ends.

We had learned to love each other all over again.

When we got married, we hadn't exchanged wedding rings. At the time, it had seemed as though we were repeating something we had already done in our previous marriages. Now, we felt it would be beautiful to have rings, as a symbol of our renewed love. We exchanged them in church, on our eighth anniversary in December, because the number *8* is the biblical symbol of new beginnings. We repeated our vows before God. To me this was important, because on our wedding day, I had not believed in God. Now, I wanted to confirm our marriage as a believer.

We didn't have our names or a date inscribed on the inside of our rings. Instead, engraved on the outside, visible for anybody who was interested, was the sign of the fish. The word *fish*, *ichthys* in Greek, was the acrostic for "Jesus Christ, God's Son, Savior." He was the basis of our marriage and, as long as we clung to him, nothing and no one would be able to destabilize it.

Almost two months later, at the end of January 2007, we once again began to discuss our roles in the church. Thiago no longer asked for our help. We went to Rome once a week just to attend the service; this, of course, wasn't strange if it hadn't been for the two-hour drive. Was it really God's will that we spend our time and energy in that way? While Jan and I were talking about it, something seemed to shift. A strong feeling grew inside of us that the time had come to begin something in our own region, to start the work for which God had called us to this part of Italy. We made an appointment with Thiago and Luiza and shared our ideas with them. They were a bit surprised, but also enthusiastic. The next Sunday, they gave us the opportunity to explain to the congregation that God had called us to serve him in Umbria. Afterwards, they prayed for us and released us with their blessing.

Bubbling with energy and ideas, we had business cards printed within a week, and within a month we had created a website. We ordered a hundred Bibles to hand out and various flyers with evangelizing texts. We acknowledged that we couldn't create a church ourselves—knowing that Jesus would do it—but we still expected a lot from our own zeal, business experience, and communication skills.

Thank God, we had no idea about the hard spiritual ground in Umbria—*terra cotta* we would come to call it—and, above all, about his plans to first mold the clay of our, still rather self-confident, egos into humbler servants who would rely on him and him only. If we had known, we might have been discouraged and tempted to give up the whole thing before even getting started.

CHAPTER NINETEEN

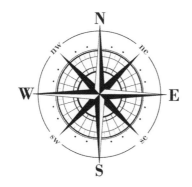

The Church

Early spring 2007

J an and I walked in Orvieto—*Urbs Vetus*—the Old City on the rock. We had prayed that God would show us where to rent a space to start a small Christian bookshop/meeting point that eventually could become a church. However, the few empty shops that had a "for rent" sign with a phone number turned out to be far too expensive.

We strolled through streets and alleys, over city walls and under archways, as usually enjoying the town's sights and surroundings. Orvieto has a rich history, which begins around 900 B.C., when the Etruscans settled on the rock. Their traces can still be found around the city. Later, its strategic position made it an attractive defensive stronghold for Romans, Barbarians, emperors and, from the eleventh century onward, popes, who used it first as a place of refuge and later annexed it to the Papal States. In fact, outside Rome, Orvieto is one of the only three cities in the world to have a papal palace; the other two are located in Viterbo and Avignon.

Orvieto had been shaped by a century-long, strong papal influence, which officially ended at the birth of the *Repubblica Italiana* in 1861. The most clearly visible legacy of that period is the *Duomo*, the 170-foot high cathedral that, by far, dominates Oriento's skyline. Historians relate that it was built by the pope's order in honor of a miracle that occurred in the city of Bolsena, about 13 miles from Orvieto. A 13th century priest doubted that the Host—the Communion bread—really turned into the body of Christ, as claimed by the Roman Catholic doctrine of transubstantiation. One day, as soon as he had spoken the words of consecration, he saw blood seep from the Host, leaving spots on the corporal, the small linen cloth on which the Host was placed. The priest brought the cloth to the pope in Orvieto, who decided that the extraordinary event deserved a great church. The construction began in 1290 A.D. and it took nearly four centuries to complete it. The *Duomo* of Orvieto, still housing the bloodstained corporal, is one of the most impressive cathedrals of all Italy, not only because of its dimensions, but also because of its façade, which is covered with sparkling, multi-colored mosaics, and ingenious sculpture work.

While wandering through Orvieto in the warm spring sun, we discussed the fact that we were about to start a new, non-denominational church in the shadow of the tangible and spiritual legacies of an age-long papacy. Would it be possible to make a breach in the stronghold?

Earlier that year, Jan had felt the Holy Spirit say that we were exactly in the heart of Italy. "Go and verify it," he had prompted. Therefore, Jan had taken a ruler and an atlas, looked up the map of Italy, and tried to determine the geographical center of the country. Italy doesn't have an easy geometrical form; it looks like a boot with a long leg and a high heel, and includes the islands of Sicily and Sardinia, which float like "deflated balls" on the west side. However, Jan managed to draw two lines that represented the length and the width of Italy and, although the map's scale was too big to pinpoint a precise location, he saw that they intersected in a point that was indeed close to Orvieto. We already knew that it had been God leading us to this part of Italy, but this revelation had added a new dimension to it. God wanted us exactly here, and now he called us to reach out to the local people, share the gospel, and plant a church right in the heart of Italy. We didn't quite understand why the geographic location was important to him, but acted in obedience.

By now, we had been in Italy for almost three years. We had learned to speak the language, not perfectly, but we managed rather well. We had come to know many Italians, their religion, and their politics. We now understood the way they discussed issues: furiously. We had made friends. We continued growing, as Christians and as a couple. Some people had said that they had never seen a more harmonious marriage than ours. Sometimes we tried to explain that it wasn't our merit, that it was only because we had invited Jesus in our relationship. We had also noticed, though, that Italian spouses had no scruples about fighting in public.

In the Netherlands, we have a proverb stating that wherever two different creeds share one pillow, the devil lies in between them. In other words, marriages with mixed beliefs will never be harmonious. Anyway, in Italy the devil seemed to exploit different political convictions even more than varying creeds to drive a wedge between partners in a marriage. *Mamma mia*! We've seen discussions mount into serious quarrels when it came to politics. Someone once explained that they talk that way only to people who are dear to them; otherwise, they wouldn't make the effort to climb over the table and grab them by the collar, metaphorically speaking of course—most of the time.

We had learned that at least one other subject of domestic quarrels could match the importance of politics: food. A favorite topic is the cooking time of the pasta. We recognized the seriousness of this issue when one of our guests even checked the pasta that I was cooking in my own kitchen. Anything other than *al dente* just won't do.

Speaking of food, another thing we had discovered about Italians was that they were particular about their dishes. Culinary creativity wasn't appreciated. Jan had once offered to make *spaghetti ai quattro formaggi* for our weekend and holiday neighbors, who were a lovely Roman family with three boys. Jan had opened our fridge, found four types of cheese and happily combined them into a sauce. When they tasted the pasta, they politely said they liked it, but also made it very clear that it wasn't the correct recipe. Jan hadn't used the right cheeses, let alone the right quantities, to make it the "real thing."

Italians also have quite different table manners. I'm not talking about their dexterity in eating their pasta, even their spaghetti, with only a fork. It was the insist-and-decline ritual that confused me. Having Italian guests for dinner, after the first portion, I always asked whether I could give them another helping. If they said no, and they always did, I removed the dish and served the next course. Over time, I had reconciled myself to the fact that, obviously, my cooking skills did not satisfy Italian requirements. On the other hand, whenever we were guests, people insisted that we take a second and, often, even a third serving. We always ended up eating too much at other people's tables, because we were afraid that they might think that we didn't appreciate their food.

One evening we had Luciano and Valeria over for dinner. I offered them a *bis*, but they declined as usual. Half a minute later, when I was about to take the dish to the kitchen, Luciano reached for the spoon and served himself a second helping. I honestly didn't know what to think but, in the end, decided that it was a compliment. Maybe my cooking was improving after all.

It took me a few years to discover the cultural difference: while we feared to offend people by declining a second helping, Italians thought it embarrassing to accept a second helping immediately, afraid to give the impression that we hadn't served them enough in the first place. I had to learn to insist when our guests declined, and to decline when our hosts insisted.

In spite of our growing understanding of the Italian people, we weren't prepared for their reactions to the fact that we were about to start a church. Frankly, I didn't feel comfortable yet when people asked us why we had come to Italy and what we were doing. Trying to explain why we didn't need to work for a living, I usually began by telling them that we lived off Jan's pension. Then I described our restoration work on the house which, during the first years, had indeed been almost a full time job. In fact, it still required a good deal of our time. I also shared our adoption plans with them, and how the procedures needed us to attend meetings and interviews. However, in the end, when people seemed satisfied with my answers and were about to change the subject, I always felt the Holy Spirit nudge me to tell the whole story.

"Well, actually we are in Italy because we felt God calling us. We are attending a Bible school through distance learning and, right now, we are starting a church."

Although people reacted in various ways, the common denominator was usually evasion and escape, often preceded by an awkward silence. The most violent reaction came from a man we met at a party. He stepped backwards so abruptly he almost fell. Although we were shocked at first, later we couldn't help but think of the reaction of the troops that came to arrest Jesus in Gethsemane, as described in the Gospel of John. "Then Jesus… said to them, 'Whom do you seek?' They answered him, 'Jesus of Nazareth.' Jesus said to them, 'I am he'… When Jesus said to them, 'I am he,' they drew back and fell to the ground."

Most Italians just didn't know one could be a Christian outside the context of the Roman Catholic Church. Even stronger, it was their conviction that someone who wasn't part of their church couldn't possibly be a Christian. Sometimes we found a person who was genuinely interested and admitted the way we lived our faith was beautifully different. Nevertheless, the concluding, shoulder-shrugging remark would often be, "Anyway, I'm Catholic." In addition—and maybe the most important reason for people's reluctance to show interest in our way of believing—openly renouncing the Catholic Church by attending non-Catholic groups of believers equaled social suicide.

In the villages of the countryside of Umbria, the Catholic Church had indeed an important role in people's life. Once I heard someone distinguish the following categories of people in the Catholic world: practicing believers who go to church, non-practicing believers who keep their faith to themselves, and the category I would have never imagined, but contained the most people, was the one of non-believing practitioners. The majority went through all the motions of religion, from infant baptism to funeral mass, without faith. God had no place in their life; tradition did. The sad thing was that people we talked to didn't even realize that Someone was missing. Yet, when we asked,

"How do you do?" the answer often was, "*Si tira avanti*," which means something like, "I get by," literally, "I'm dragging myself through life." Their face expressed a mix of fatalism and futility as they mentioned family problems, failing health, or financial troubles, seeing no ray of hope in a dark world. Nevertheless, whether they believed or not, the one thing they didn't worry about was where they would go after death. They were taught that the sacraments of the Roman Catholic tradition impart grace and are necessary for salvation, so these formed their ticket to heaven, with or without the intermediate station of the purgatory.

In time, we learned not to focus on our activities when we explained what we were doing in Italy, but on Jesus and on our relationship with him. We learned to listen to the Holy Spirit and discern the opportunities to share God's transforming love with them.

During the first months of our attempts to begin a church, we went often to Orvieto to evangelize. We didn't feel led to carry out the "cold method," that is, stopping people abruptly in their tracks, handing them a flyer, and trying to trap them into a talk about God. We always prayed beforehand that God would lead us to the people he had in mind, or them to us. We prayed that friendships and relationships would be the vehicle of God's words of love and truth.

One morning, we stopped to look at the shop window of a local artist. It was full of gray, depressing paintings with many references to the cross. Wondering whether these expressed the painter's faith, we decided that he definitely needed to hear the Good News, so we entered the shop. The man we met inside was friendly and cheerful, but he wasn't the artist. Ciro became a good friend of ours, respectful of our faith but, unfortunately, didn't believe in God.

In May, a man named Corrado contacted us, because he was interested in our work. After we met him, he accepted our offer to do some Bible studies. For lack of a meeting room, Jan sat a couple of times with him on the steps of the *Duomo* but, after one particular session in which Jan explained the necessity to "repent and believe in Jesus" in order to be reconciled with God, Corrado cancelled the next appointment.

A young woman, who was a member of a Catholic charismatic group in Orvieto, was interested as well. We counseled her and did some Bible studies with her. Although she valued our pastoral care, she didn't join us.

Sometimes we thought that God simply wanted us to bear witness to the living God and bring people closer to Jesus, without forming a church.

Although we felt God's guidance in everything we did, we also recognized that we needed to link into a greater network, not only to have fellowship with Christians who had more experience than we did, but also for the sake of accountability. That is why we met with Marcus and Adele again that spring. They answered many questions and greatly encouraged us. We told them we wanted to submit to their apostolic authority, because we felt that it was God's way of making us missionaries. They laid hands on us and prayed for our ministry. Marcus also invited us for a meeting they called "Equip," to be held at the end of June. This gathering, consisting of three days of profound teaching, worshiping, and praying, was balm for our souls. It was wonderful to get to know many people from all over the world, all of whom had purposefully come to Italy to teach those forming new churches, and to encourage church leaders, to "hold up their hands."

Afterwards, two South African couples, leading elders of a 200-member church, felt they should come to our house for two days. We talked, prayed, and worshiped together, and God used them to speak into our lives and ministry. One of their recommendations was to start the church right away in our house. We were not to wait for a suitable space in Orvieto, nor even for people to attend!

Therefore, as of the first Sunday in July 2007, we held a weekly celebration service with worship and preaching, in Italian of course. Jan preached the Word that God gave him, and I led the worship. The electronic organ lessons I had taken as a child and the singing lessons I had done as an adult turned out to be a good preparation. Our little programmable keyboard accompanied the songs, and a second-hand overhead projector showed the lyrics on one of the walls of our living room. It was attended by Jan, myself, and Jesus.

In spite of our efforts, with an occasional exception, it would remain just the three of us until December 2008. That was when we would finally welcome our child.

CHAPTER TWENTY

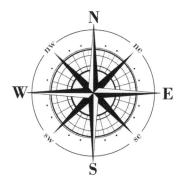

The Tree

Sardinia, October 2007

"*I* see a tree, a big green tree."

The woman hesitated before continuing. I looked at her back while she faced the wall in front of her and I felt her trying to see and hear more from God.

"I don't know," she said, "It's just this tree."

She turned round and faced me. "Oh it's you! Maybe it means that you'll carry a lot of fruit for Jesus."

She hadn't known for whom she had prayed. The exercise of blindly prophesying was part of a weeklong conference Jan and I attended. The week consisted of learning about God's loving heart, searching the condition of our own hearts, and praying that included listening to God. The first time we had to pray and receive something from God for another person, I had been apprehensive. Was it actually possible to solicit words from God and, moreover, would *I* be able to hear them? We had been seeking God's presence in worship and prayer for almost an hour, and then the leader of the conference said that we were to pray in tongues to open our spirit and share the thoughts or images that flooded our mind. I was amazed when people—me included—exchanged a seemingly never-ending stream of encouraging words and visions.

During my walk with Jesus, almost three years now, I had learned that we could hear from God. I had read several books on it—for example, *Can you hear God?* by Joyce Sibthorpe—and devoured the testimonies. Almost every day, when I had my time alone with God, during which I worshiped, prayed, and read my Bible, I had tried to listen as well. I kept a journal in which I wrote down my prayers and God's answers to them—in practice or through his word. Only very seldom was I able to write down something I *thought* he had said or shown to me. During that week in Sardinia, it became clear: God *always* communicates with us, but we need to open our spiritual eyes and ears, and believe.

Now, at the end of the conference, we shared the last prophetic moment. I received the image of the big green tree in my heart and trusted God that its meaning would become clear.

Earlier that year, in April, after six months of information sessions, psychological interviews, and an ultimate interview with the Juvenile Court's president, we were formally approved as adoptive parents. We had a year to accomplish the next step, which was devoted to selecting an *ente*, an authorized foreign adoption agency that would include us in their database until they selected us as the best couple for a certain child who needed a family. How do you choose one, and only one, agency among almost seventy?

For the sake of distance, we tried to focus on agencies in the center of Italy. At first, we visited some agencies together, but we didn't feel any base for a relationship with them. To save time and money, I went to some other information sessions on my own. It wasn't easy to make a decision, and there were moments when we almost quarreled. I was ready to do whatever was necessary, to go anywhere, and for any length of time, in order to have my baby. Jan was more practical. "We cannot leave for three months to go to South America for the adoption! We must choose an agency that represents countries that don't require a long stay abroad."

I was desperate and said that, if it was God's will, it could be organized. But I realized that it would be difficult, and maybe it wasn't what God's wanted.

Additionally, there was the age factor. Some agencies were rather rude when I told them that I was forty-five and my husband fifty-six. Yet another problem was that most agencies refused a gender preference and were outraged about our even inquiring, "Because you don't choose your child." Obviously, they were right, but they didn't even want to know *why* it was important to us.

In our hearts, our child was growing. At the start of the adoption procedure, she was very young, under two years old. However, as we heard about children in orphanages who saw younger kids being adopted and leaving, while they stayed and realized that, perhaps, they would never have a mom and dad, my child grew older. At a certain moment, we both felt that Africa was the native continent of our child, and Ethiopia stood out in our hearts.

Time after time, I found myself sitting at our table with the list of agencies, scrutinizing their locations, the countries they represented, the number of adoptions they had mediated in the last years, the average waiting time, and the length of stay in the countries to complete the procedure. We had contacted most of the agencies in central Italy, including Rome. I had even checked with agencies in the Netherlands to determine whether it would be possible to adopt through them and, if yes, what their waiting times would be. However, according to Dutch law, we would never qualify for adoption, both being forty-five or older.

Then one afternoon, not long after our Sardinia conference, while browsing through the multi-page list once again, my eyes latched onto an agency in Milan. It was authorized for adoptions of Ethiopian children and it was one of the bigger agencies; this was an advantage in terms of experience and reliability. Sighing, I was about to discard it as an option, because I knew that we would need to attend multiple meetings and interviews, and Milan was simply too far away. All of a sudden, I saw that they also had an office in Rome. I picked up the phone, called the Roman number, and heard a friendly woman respond. I explained our situation and started right away with the most important question, "I have contacted many other agencies and most of them say we're too old. What do you think?"

She answered that, in her opinion, our age didn't matter if the Juvenile Court had approved us as adoptive parents. My second question was, "Would you allow us to express a preference for a girl?"

Her answer was cautious. "Well, normally we don't accept a preference, but we can talk about your reasons for it."

We made an appointment. Jan and I decided that I would go alone to explore the possibilities.

When I arrived in the agency's office in a *palazzo* in Rome, I found the same friendly woman who welcomed me and another couple to the information meeting. She calmly explained the possibilities and procedures with the agency, making it clear that waiting times for small children were long, but much shorter for older ones, because fewer couples were open to adopting older children. She reassured me again that our age wasn't a problem at all.

At the end, she handed out an information package, including the agency's magazine. Its name really stood out, I couldn't have missed it even if I had wanted to do so. Using the full width of the front page and printed in green ink, there it was, *L'Albero Verde*—"The Green Tree." We had found our agency.

The next few months we had several meetings and interviews in Rome in preparation for the adoption. Although the agency's representatives explained that their starting point was always what was best for a given child—searching for the best parents for a child rather than looking out for the ideal child for a couple—in the last interview with the psychologist, Isabella, we talked about our personal preferences. We explained our situation with Jan having two sons and our attraction to Ethiopia. She said she understood, but told us that they wouldn't guarantee anything. "For example, if we were to propose a boy from Vietnam for whom you would make the best parents in our database, would you consider adopting him?"

We trusted that we were right in the middle of God's will, so we answered with a whole-hearted, "Yes, we would."

I realized that, during the procedure, not only the image of the child had changed, but also my attitude towards adoption. What had begun as my own desire for a child had evolved into a deep longing to fulfill a child's need. Furthermore, the initial idea that adopting was "Plan B" in family making had grown into the strong belief that it is God's primary way to create his family. As God's Word says, "He predestined us for adoption as sons through Jesus Christ, according to the purpose of his will." We ourselves, born into an earthly family, had become children of our heavenly Father by adoption.

After the last interview in January 2008, the waiting period began. Until then, we had been able to contribute to the procedure. There had been decisions to make, documents to gather, and meetings to attend. Now we couldn't do anything and just had to wait, without knowing for how long. A few months, a year, two years? We were sure that God's hand was in the procedure, but we were also well aware that God's timing is hardly ever ours. I felt pregnant without knowing the length of the gestation period.

In May, Jan's youngest son married. A good friend of ours, Cor, had come from the Netherlands to stay with us for a couple weeks. He was not only wonderful company, but also a great handyman and he helped us to give our building activities a boost. In addition, because Cor was willing to care for the animals for a few days, Jan and I were able to go to the Netherlands together, to attend the joyful event.

While we lingered at Rome airport, waiting for our flight to Amsterdam, I checked my mobile phone and noticed a lost call. I didn't recognize the number, but immediately thought of the adoption agency. Calling the unfamiliar number, it turned out to be them indeed; they wanted us to come to their headquarters in Milan that week, "to evaluate an adoption possibility." I felt like taking flight without the plane, because this meant that they had found our baby! For one moment, I was inclined to cancel our trip to the Netherlands, but then reason took over, and we postponed the appointment until the week after the wedding.

We really enjoyed the short, festive holiday together, during which Jan became the proud father of a married son and a beautiful daughter-in-law, but we were also looking forward to the meeting in Milan. Would I finally become a mother?

CHAPTER TWENTY-ONE

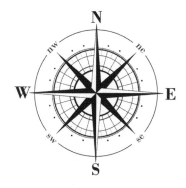

The Child

Milan, May 21, 3 p.m.

*A*fter several long train trips filled with delays, we found ourselves in a room with Isabella, the adoption agency's psychologist with whom we had spoken before. She checked briefly with us whether we still wished to adopt—"yes, of course"—and then began to talk cautiously about a little girl in Ethiopia. Next to me, I heard Jan thank God under his breath; he had been praying for a girl at least a hundred times a day.

Isabella told us that the child, whose estimated age was seven years, had lost both parents, had lived in an orphanage in Addis Ababa for more than a year now, and was waiting for a family. She shared what she knew about the girl and then asked us, "Do you want to adopt her?"

We didn't have to think, we didn't even look at each other. We just said, very convinced, "Yes, we want her to become our daughter."

Only God could have arranged this, so we knew that this little one was to be ours, and that his blessing would be all over us. Her name was Aisha.

The two pictures that Isabella showed us after our positive reaction were heartbreaking. They were taken at two different occasions, about six months apart. The first showed a beautiful girl with a lovely smile, light brown skin, beaming eyes, and brown braids that were lying flat on her head. She was dressed in a dark blue school uniform that consisted of a long skirt, a sports shirt, and a woolen sweater. Every garment was at least two sizes too big. On her chest shone a silvery pendant in the form of a cross.

On the second, more recent picture, it was difficult even to recognize that it was the same girl. Her smile was forced, her eyes seemed tired, her hair was thin, and her skin dull. She was wearing the same clothes all right, but we noticed a swollen belly protruding from beneath her sweater. It was clear that living in the orphanage wasn't doing her any good. Isabella explained that the changes were probably the result of vitamin deficiency.

"When can we go and get her?" I asked, hoping that Isabella would say something like, "next week" or, at the latest, "next month."

Instead, she said, "Well, if everything goes according to plan, the procedure in Ethiopia will take about six months, so you will meet her in, let's see… in November or December."

My hope sank. Our daughter was suffering in an orphanage, and we couldn't do anything to change this. When we said goodbye to Isabella, her parting words were, "This is the strangest adoption I've ever mediated." She was out of the door before we could ask her what she meant.

Early menopause or not, the maternal hormones were raging through my body. After we got home, we called Sabrina, our new contact person at the agency, who was responsible for African adoptions, and said that we wanted to pay for vitamins–not just for Aisha but for all the kids in the orphanage. Could she organize that please? Sabrina laughed, because she recognized the thirst for action so characteristic of parents during the waiting period. She assured me that the health of the children in the orphanage was the agency's responsibility and advised me to concentrate on the paperwork required to continue the procedure.

In fact, they had given us a long list of documents we needed to gather: birth certificates, written references from neighbors and friends, marriage certificate, income statement, certificates of moral conduct… The agency would have all documents translated into English and send them to their contact person in Addis Ababa. This person would then present the file to the responsible Ethiopian court, which would decide whether we could adopt Aisha. The sooner we collected the documents, the sooner the court would process our case, and the sooner we could go to get our daughter.

I was intent on setting a paperwork record, but it took me three whole weeks. Some of the mills of the government turned slowly. For example, one official had been too busy to help me right away. To convince me of this dreadful fact, she dragged me to her work place, so that I could see the piles of papers waiting to be dealt with. The tears in my eyes, while I explained that her work was the last link in the paperwork chain that allowed us to go ahead in the adoption procedure, didn't affect her decision to put our documents at the bottom of one the piles.

On June 13, I finally put the required documents in a box and added a few small, but carefully chosen, presents for Aisha: a brown, cuddly teddy bear with a big red heart in its paws that said, "I love you," a children's watch, a tiny mobile in the form of a ladybug with tinkling sticks, and a small red cloth bag with purple dots and a zipper, in which we put the watch and the mobile. We prayed that our daughter would feel the love that we had poured into each of the presents, that it would help her to bear the life in the orphanage and make it through the long months before we would see one another.

Not that we were twiddling our thumbs in the meantime. We had a bathroom and a child's room under construction.

CHAPTER TWENTY-TWO

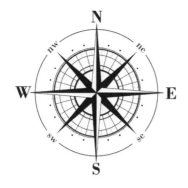

The Vision

Sunday, June 22, 2008

"Now this was the dream I had a couple of weeks ago," said the petite girl from South Africa. "I saw a huge heart. In the center of the heart was a door that opened and, in its opening, stood Jesus in a radiant light. He reached out his arm and said, '*Vieni a me*'—'Come to me'. The peculiar thing is that he spoke Italian; this led me to the conclusion that he was talking to Italian people."

Jan reacted, and I could hear the emotion in his voice. "Your dream really speaks to me. It's a strong confirmation that God, in his love, wants to reach out to the Italians from here, where we are, in the heart of Italy."

The girl, named Alisa, smiled shyly, while her young husband Ben watched her with love and pride in his eyes. They were our guests after we had all attended the second NCMI Equip meeting in Tuscany, which had been a huge blessing again. Now we found ourselves in the big meeting room Jan and I had constructed in the ex-stable, under the living quarters of our house. We had left the walls as natural as possible and put in a ceiling with thick wooden beams. A long table, with fourteen chairs around it, stood in the middle of the room on the terracotta floor tiles. A white sheet showed the projected text of the last worship song we had sung during our celebration. We thanked God for his promises for the heart of Italy and for his progressive revelation of what he wanted to do through us.

The years 2004 and 2005 had been years of beginnings. We had arrived in Italy, learned the language, and gotten acquainted with the Italian culture. I gave my life to Jesus, we both were baptized, Jan initiated ministering while I started my journey with God, which led me through—and out of—a spiritual desert. We began our distance Bible school with the NCMI.

In 2006, we grew a lot through studying and helping the Brazilian church in Rome. We also committed ourselves to adopting a child.

Then 2007 had been the year of the start of a new church, of friendships with people in the NCMI network, and further personal growth. We had been relating to many Italians, witnessing of Christ, making new friends, but until now nobody had made the decision to give their life to Jesus or decided to join us during the celebration meetings at our house. To be honest, we were very discouraged at times, seeing no fruit at all. We were sowing, but we didn't see any seeds germinate, let alone any harvest that we could we reap. Still, we were faithfully holding our Sunday celebration meetings, worshiping Jesus, and teaching his Word.

Many times, we had prayed for direction, for divine strategy to reach more people. God's promises were numerous: we would be called "Repairers of the Breach," as in chapter 58 of Isaiah, God would wake up and shake the people to draw them to him (Haggai), and we would have so many spiritual children that we would need to expand our premises (Isaiah, chapter 54).

This year, 2008, had initiated with fresh revelation for our local ministry, as if God wanted to encourage us not to give up. A wonderful couple from South Africa, Norah and Rick, had come to Italy for three weeks, around the turn of the year, to encourage us. Actually, they had felt God saying that he wanted them to come to Italy to serve him while helping us. One day, when we worshiped together, God showed Norah in a vision that we had silvery powder on our heads and shoulders. At first, we thought this meant that God would soon anoint us, so that we could become more effective in our work for him. However, later Norah received this verse in Psalm 115, "Not to us, O LORD, not to us, but to your name give glory, for the sake of your steadfast love and your faithfulness!"

Additional study of the use of silver in the Bible revealed that it refers to atonement and purification. In the book of Exodus, we read that, when the people of Israel wandered in the desert, God gave Moses precise instructions how to build a place for worship called the tabernacle. The supporting construction of the tabernacle was a wooden frame consisting of vertical boards and horizontal bars to connect the boards. Each board was to stand on two silver sockets, made from the silver that the people of Israel had given during a census as ransom money, "that it may bring the people of Israel to remembrance before the LORD, so as to make atonement for your lives." God wanted the people to remember that their strength came from him and not from how many they were. Pride in numbers should never replace dependence upon God.

Just as the silver sockets were the bases of the tabernacle, where God's presence was to descend while his people was wandering in the wilderness, so should our complete dependence on God be the basis of anything we intended to build for him during our journey of forming a church. In this phase, God was not asking us to give account of the number of people who had joined us. Instead, he wanted to purify our hearts from any boasting in our own efforts and from hurt pride that we hadn't succeeded yet in gathering a church. We had to be saturated with the realization that only God's grace of redemption would form the church. We depended completely and totally upon him, and the glory of anything great would be his, not ours.

God was using our walk to our spiritual destination—the realization of his promises—to teach us to focus on him. Just as he had taught me during my first year as a Christian that, to get out of my depression, I should not lean on my own understanding, but cling to him, he now wanted us to be aware that forming a church didn't depend on our skills, but on his grace and mercy.

God continued talking to us. After Rick and Norah went back to South Africa, Jan received another confirmation that we had to acknowledge God's sovereignty, summarized in this Bible verse, "So then it depends not on human will or exertion, but on God, who has mercy."

One morning in January, just before waking up, I dreamt that I saw two small boats navigating calmly towards me over smooth water. One boat had eight people in it, the other thirty. When I woke up, I knew in a flash that the boats represented two moments for our local church. The boat with eight people had something to do with the beginning of the church at our place, and the one with thirty people represented the moment at which we would begin to send people to other towns to start new church groups. Later, when Jan prayed over this dream, it occurred to him that *8* was the symbol for new beginnings, and he felt that God said our church would be the beginning of a new movement for him. The number *30*, which can be seen as a symbol for maturity in ministry, indicated that God would allow us to expand our ministry at the right moment. For either occasion, we needed to have patience. They would surely come but, as the pace of the boats and the calm water reflected, in God's perfect timing.

In March, I prayed to God to show me the way to grow our local church. While I opened my spirit for his answer, I saw myself in a wooded forest. A long strand of wool on waist height ran crisscross through the woods, twisting around trees, and intersecting itself in many places. Arriving at the edge of the forest, the thread made a straight line to a hilltop town that I saw in the distance and, from that town to another hilltop town and so on, connecting many towns like beads on a string. God's message was, "Cling to me and follow me in trust, even if you don't understand where I am leading you. In the end, you will reach the destination I have set before you. People in many Italian cities will surrender to me and work in unity to advance my Kingdom." The Bible verse I felt led to confirmed God's guidance in difficult, seemingly confusing situations. "And your ears shall hear a word behind you, saying, 'This is the way, walk in it,' when you turn to the right or when you turn to the left."

Another time I heard God say, "I'm coming, be patient," and an image popped up in my mind: a horseman, a king, rode on a path through flourishing trees and bushes. It was spring, and the air was pregnant with the promise of fruit. The King was on his way to fulfill his promises of the harvest.

Now God was confirming through our young South African friend Alisa that we were walking in his will. God would use us in wonderful ways, but he also said, "Wait on me," as in Isaiah 64. It would be for Jesus to build the church, not for us. Yes, we had to make ourselves available and carry out his commission to preach the gospel, to sow the seed, but we couldn't convince people to turn to him. Only his Holy Spirit could make the seed germinate and the sprouts grow. In the meantime, he was helping us to prepare our hearts to be able to conquer the Promised Land and face the new challenges we would find there.

After Alisa told us her dream about the heart that Sunday, she also shared an impression that she received while we had praised and worshiped together. She said that, during our worship, she had felt vibrations of the Holy Spirit going into the surrounding area, as ever-increasing concentric circles rippling out from the spot where a pebble hits the water in a pond. "I think the Holy Spirit is saying that worship moves something in the spiritual realm as a war tactic to set people free," she added and referred to the book of Acts, where it is written that Paul and Silas, being imprisoned, prayed and sang to God. As they sang, an earthquake shook the foundations of the prison, opened its doors and loosed the chains of all the prisoners.

What I didn't know was that, after Alisa had shared her dream about the heart, Jan prayed God to confirm that all of this had something to do with *our* ministry. During the following night, Alisa had another dream in which she saw me firing a pistol with my right hand, pointing it upwards with a stretched arm, as if it were a starting gun for a track meet. The shot set our house on fire, but the flames didn't consume it.

When Jan heard the dream, he immediately said that it confirmed his vision of God doing something extraordinary in the heart of Italy, and added that it referred to our musical worship. Normally, when I play the keyboard, I use only my left hand to play the chords and let the keyboard produce the backing rhythm and accompaniment. Often, I lift up my right arm in worship, a posture that Jan saw reflected in Alisa's dream. He concluded that our worship was important in God's plan for Umbria; it would release the anointing to draw the Italian people to Jesus.

To be honest, I wasn't so sure about all these words about me worshiping. Although I loved to sing and worship, I thought that the quality of what I was doing was low. After all, my musical talents weren't that great, and the sound that came out of the keyboard wasn't that inspiring. One of my prayers since we had started our home church was that real musicians would join us so that they could take over the musical leadership.

What was God telling us? That it didn't matter how it sounded, as long as we worshiped? That it was the heart that counted, not the musical talents? And why was it important anyway that we actually sang songs, why couldn't we just worship without sound, without music? Was it because we did it together, in unity?

The last week of June, while we continued working on Aisha's room, we pondered all information that God had spoken to us through our South African friends and tried to merge it with the pieces that God had already given us to create one overall vision for our ministry in Italy.

The first of July, Sabrina of the adoption agency called us with good and bad news. The bad news was that Aisha had suffered from pneumonia, and had been in the hospital; the really good news was that she had recovered well and was back in the orphanage. Furthermore, the local psychologist had informed her that she was to be adopted. Her reaction had been a spontaneous, "I love you Mommy and Daddy!" The picture that Sabrina sent us by email was proof of her health and joy, showing a big, beaming smile and sparkling eyes.

Other good news was that our translated documents were at the Ethiopian embassy in Rome, waiting for authentication. But the other bad news was that, from mid-July, the Ethiopian court would close for two months. Our documents wouldn't make it there in time.

CHAPTER TWENTY-THREE

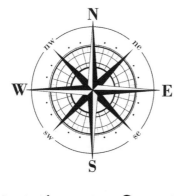

The Wait

*T*he summer of 2008 was particularly hot. The apathy of long afternoons in the scorching Italian heat, with the characteristic monotonous sound of the cicada song, seemed to reflect the immobility of both our church and the adoption procedure. Our construction work slowed down as well. It was as if all activity had succumbed to the high temperatures, waiting for autumn, when cooler air would raise it from its temporary paralysis.

There were some moments of refreshment though. Our morale was invigorated when we received more pictures of Aisha, along with a psychological report stating that she was a cheerful girl who was developing well, both physically and socially, and didn't show any sign of stress. She was a real chatterbox and had liked our pictures in the photo album we had made for her. Further, the report stated, "Aisha has a positive attitude towards adoption. She has even begun to ask questions like, 'When will they come here?' She has also made a drawing for her family, which is attached to this report."

The drawing brought tears to my eyes. It was a house with a path leading up to the front door. Flowers, hearts, and her name adorned the area around the house. Two hearts, one on each side of the path, contained the words *I love you*. Our own hearts overflowed with love for the child we were bringing into our home but, until she arrived, we could only pour it into buying girl's clothes and in planning the design of her room, which would be cream-colored with red and pink accessories. A real "girly" room. Sometimes I asked myself, *What if she is a tough girl, who likes cars and football?* But then quickly discarded the thought.

The Dutch climate brought me some literal cooling, because I went to the Netherlands to help my mother move into a nursing home. After her recovery from the heart surgery four years ago, she had gone back to her own little house. However, her mental capacities had gradually diminished. I had brought her to Italy twice for a short holiday, so that she would know where we had started our new lives. The photo albums I had made of these occasions helped to remind her that she had a daughter in Italy.

The people from the church The Well had indeed kept their promise. They made it possible for my mother to attend the Sunday morning services, and she thrived in the gentle atmosphere. In addition, one lady, Lea, came to visit my mother almost every week. In the first year, when I spoke to her on the phone, she told me how she had chatted with my mother at the kitchen table.

"How is it possible that all the people in the church are so friendly? That they are always smiling and always say nice things?" my mother wondered.

"That is because they carry Jesus in their hearts. They are Christians," Lea answered and, when my mother's face lit up, she continued, "Would you like to become a Christian too?"

"Oh, yes!" my mother exclaimed. Whereupon Lea had led my mother in a simple prayer to ask for forgiveness and accept Jesus. My mother understood and repeated every single word.

Now, two years later, her dementia made it too dangerous for her to live on her own. My brother had turned off the gas valve, because we were afraid she would set the house on fire. She would go for a walk and get lost, put the thermostat of the central heating on 90 degrees, and let anybody enter the house; this, in fact, had resulted in a theft.

When we received the news that the nursing home had a room available, my brother was on holiday on Curaçao, my sister-in-law's native island–so it was up to my sister and me. I brought my mother one last time to The Well, and the pastor allowed us to thank and greet the church community. My mother beamed as she stood in front, next to her daughter "who lives in Italy."

Elisabeth and I managed to move my mother and part of her furniture within two days, but I had to come back a second time, because the three of us wanted to empty our family home together, decide what to throw away, what to give away, what to keep, and who would keep it. Thank God, it all worked out in complete harmony, and I really enjoyed spending time with my family.

It wasn't until the first week of September that Sabrina informed us that the Ethiopian court finally had accepted our file. The setback was that the court would re-open only at the end of the month. However, with the good news and the lower temperatures, we were motivated to pick up speed and continue working on Aisha's room.

Tensions rose as the end of September approached, but we had to wait until October 5 for the news that the court in Addis Ababa had planned the hearing for our case, in which the agency's contact person would represent us. The date: October 27.

Our pregnancy symptoms increased. With every girl aged between five and ten we saw, we asked ourselves whether Aisha would be shorter or taller, and we had to control ourselves not to bellow out to the accompanying parents that soon we would have a daughter too. I carried Aisha's pictures in my bag, which I showed—solicited or unsolicited—to all friends and acquaintances I met. I surfed the Internet to read other people's stories of adopting a child from Ethiopia and tried to put myself in their position. I downloaded a full language course of Amharic, Aisha's mother tongue, but, to be honest, I wasn't sure whether I would be able to study all 519 pages. While building, plastering, and painting, we dreamed about how her voice would sound, how she would smell, how her face would look in her sleep, what food she would like, and what activities we would do together. In my daydreams, I mainly played with my daughter. I had bought colored scrapbook paper, glitter pens, craft scissors, and face paints, and I had saved bundles of paintbrushes that had belonged to my father. Jan was dreaming of reading, telling her stories, and letting her swing on the big wooden swing he planned to make for her. And both of us dreamed of endless chattering.

On October 27, the telephone rang at 10:30 a.m. A happy Sabrina gave us the news we had been waiting for so long: the court in Addis Ababa had approved of our adoption. As of that moment and according to Ethiopian law, Aisha was our daughter! We almost exploded with joy and called all of our family and friends to let off steam.

At the end of November, we would meet our daughter. Finally. The wait was almost over.

CHAPTER TWENTY-FOUR

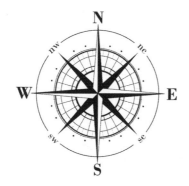

The Family

Rome Airport,
November 24, midnight

The departure of our 8-hour flight to Addis Ababa with Ethiopian Airlines had been planned for 5 minutes past midnight but, unfortunately, it was delayed for two and a half hours. Occasionally, we talked a bit with our new friends from Milan, Piero and Marina, with whom we would travel and be hotel room neighbors during the coming ten days. They were to adopt three kids from the same orphanage in Addis Ababa, a girl of Aisha's age with her two brothers, one younger, the other older. However, most of the time, Jan and I just waited and tried to rest on the uncomfortable airport chairs, tired but too excited to fall asleep.

We had won the race against time to prepare Aisha's bedroom, even though we flew to Ethiopia almost a week earlier than expected. The next day we would meet Aisha and take her to the hotel, where we stayed until our return to Italy on December 3.

My thoughts went back to three days ago, to the last interview with Isabella, the agency's psychologist. She had shown us Aisha's latest pictures, taken only a week ago. The braids were gone! Short curls now framed her lovely smiling face. Isabella explained that it probably had been difficult to untangle her frizzy hair, and that they had cut it in anticipation of the adoption.

Furthermore, Isabella had tried to prepare us for the meeting with our daughter, a moment we had lived at least a thousand times in our daydreams, but not in the way that she described. The worst-case scenario was that Aisha would panic, refuse to see us, and not want to leave the orphanage with us. The advice in this situation was to stay calm and try again the next day. Another possibility was that Aisha would "fall in love" with one of us and completely ignore the other one. In this case, we were not to force anything, but to be loving and patient, simply remaining available for her attentions. A completely different reaction could be that she would show socially desirable behavior, trying to do anything to please us, afraid of being left behind otherwise. Heartbreaking and unnatural but, as a beginning, this scenario seemed less difficult than the other two scenarios. We had prayed that God would prepare her heart for the meeting, and that he would help her to put her trust in us.

At the end of our meeting with Isabella, we asked her what she had meant last time when she said, "This is the strangest adoption I've ever mediated." Her answer was, "Normally I follow a precise procedure, in which I evaluate several couples to find the one that best matches the needs of a given child. However, when I received Aisha's file on my desk, I just knew that it had to be you. I never even considered any other couple."

We were amazed. Jan asked her, "Do you realize that you followed the prompting of God's Holy Spirit?"

She smiled, a bit embarrassed. It was obvious that she didn't believe him. Nevertheless, we knew that God's hand was on this adoption and that he would be with us—all three of us—faithfully, from the very first day.

We landed at the Bole International Airport in Addis Ababa at 10:30 a.m., after a long night with a couple of catnaps. When we had successfully gone through the practicalities of getting a visa, going through passport control, and claiming our luggage, we met Dario, the agency's contact person, and Yonas, the Ethiopian driver of the agency van that would transport us through the city during our stay.

Our first trip, from the airport to the hotel, gave us an overwhelming impression of extremes: wealth and poverty, health and illness, modern buildings and slums, cars and animals. In addition, we saw beautiful people and radiant colors, as the city's noise and chaos engulfed us. We were exhausted, but still excited and expectant. Piero cried openly and, while tears streamed down his face, he explained with a smile that he was a native Sicilian and that, in Sicily, men were more in touch with their emotions.

The meeting at the orphanage had been planned for the morning but, because of our delay, it was postponed until the afternoon. Then, after a short shower and our first Ethiopian lunch–delicious *injera*–we finally headed to the orphanage. Nervousness had set in with all four of us. Piero shed more tears, Marina and I giggled, and Jan shouted things like, "Aisha, here we come!"

Fifteen minutes later, we drove up a hill, passed through a gate, and parked the van. Jan and I walked hand in hand, while we followed Dario and Yonas. In my free hand, I carried a bag with some small presents for Aisha. After walking up a long stairway, we arrived in a courtyard, where Sister Reinolda, the principal of the orphanage, was waiting for us. She greeted us with the words, "The kids were ready and waiting for you this morning at 10 o'clock!"

We apologized and explained about the flight problems, a bit taken back by her reproach. Still grumbling under her breath, she led us into a small room with two old sofas, a chair, a television, and piles of crates filled with toys. Piero and Marina sat down on one sofa, while Jan and I seated ourselves on the other. Sister Reinolda sat on the chair and told us that she had sent someone to fetch the children. While we waited, we exchanged some civilities but, at this point, we weren't concentrating on the conversation. All four of us focused on the door through which our children would enter our lives. Another fifteen minutes later, we noticed that something was happening outside, and someone said, "Here they come!"

Four small children were ushered into the room, and one of them was Aisha. Our Aisha. I recognized her immediately. That lovely face. Somebody had dressed her in a pink and white striped T-shirt under a yellow pinafore dress that was too tight, dark grey tights with red flowers, and orange sandals. She was visibly uncomfortable in those clothes and as nervous as we were. The uncertainty was drawn on her little face. But she recognized us as well.

While the other three walked into the waiting arms of Piero and Marina, Aisha hugged first me and then Jan. Timidly. We hugged her back, but let her go when she withdrew. Sister Reinolda asked her who we were, and she called us dutifully Mommy and Daddy. We looked at one another, adoptive parents and child, a bit ill at ease and not really knowing what to do next. We wanted to grab her and hold her tightly all day long, but we didn't want to force Aisha into something for which she wasn't ready. Therefore, we gave her the presents, which she calmly unpacked. Her face lit up, and a little smile broke through, when she discovered a doll and a comb. She began combing the doll's hair right away.

I tried to communicate with her, a bit in English, a bit in Italian, and using a lot of sign language. When I asked her to show me around in the house, she willingly stood up and gave me a guided tour. She led the way, more secure now and with a certain pride in her step. Jan followed us with a video camera.

We saw staircases, long corridors, and her bedroom with six cots and five bunk beds. Aisha explained that the children slept in twos in each bed. And we saw rooms filled with them, many children, all lovely and beautiful children, who looked at us, their eyes radiating a mix of curiosity and desperate longing. Who were these people who were about to take away one of their peers? Would anyone ever come to adopt them?

Back in the room with Sister Reinolda, we asked the principal about Aisha's daily routine and her habits, trying to figure out as much as possible about her. Everything went well until we began to talk about food. Reinolda teased Aisha, who was sitting next to me, about the fact that she didn't like milk. "You will need to drink milk with your new family, you know that."

I saw Aisha pout, lower her gaze, put an arm over her eyes, and suddenly a big round tear slowly rolled down her cheek. The scene was the catalyst to release my full maternal instinct. Letting go of all caution, I pulled her onto my lap and wrapped my arms around her, holding her closely. Her body, too small for her age, pressed against mine, tense.

At that moment, nothing else mattered. It was just me holding her, gently rocking, and whispering comforting words in her ear. She cried, whimpering softly, probably not only because she was afraid to drink milk, but also because she needed to vent the stress of this long-awaited day. She absorbed every drop of affection I poured into her, and slowly but surely, I felt her relax. God's hand was all around us as he knitted our hearts together, making us mother and daughter. My eyes crossed with Jan's while he was filming us, and I knew: all was well.

When we left the orphanage half an hour later, Aisha walked ahead of us, determined and confident. Her new life had begun, and ours as well. We were a family. We were complete now, ready for whatever new beginning God had in mind for us.

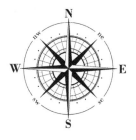

Epilogue

November 2013

O bviously, this story doesn't end at the moment we became a family. It was the beginning of something incredibly beautiful. As a family, we have become strong, even stronger than we were before as a couple. It is as God says, "And though a man might prevail against one who is alone, two will withstand him—a threefold cord is not quickly broken."

In the first place, we are a family for Aisha, one that will guide her as she grows into the woman her Creator intended her to be. However, we also form a team for Christ that wouldn't be complete without her. God has already spoken to us more than once through her dreams and her visions, sometimes simply to confirm that his hand is on her, other times to convey a message to us. I'll share two examples.

In the first year she was with us, she sometimes fell asleep during Jan's preaching on Sunday morning (because she didn't yet understand all of the Italian, not because Jan is a boring preacher, of course). In one occasion, Jan had talked about how important it is always to remain in God's presence, even in difficult times. He spoke about how, rather than running away from him in disbelief, fear, or shame, we should run towards him to find hope, security, and restoration. At the end of the sermon, Aisha, who had been comfortably sitting on my lap, her little head in my neck, woke up with a big yawn and said she'd had a dream.

"I was flying with Jesus in the air. We went from our house to the center of Poggio. While we flew above the village, I saw that some people were happy to see him, but others reacted with so much fear that it scared me. I wanted to go home immediately, so I left Jesus, but I couldn't find our house without him. I was alone and very afraid."

We marveled at the ways of the Holy Spirit; the message of the dream reflected the one Jan had shared (and more).

A year or so later, we were in the Land Rover on our way to a friend for homemade pizza. We had put on worship music, and were singing along, lustily and joyfully, to Justin Rizzo's song, "Glory will cover the earth." Meanwhile, we drove across a hill, between vineyards and olive groves, and a panoramic view over the valley opened before us in the twilight. Suddenly, Aisha stopped singing and said, "I saw beams of light coming from heaven, as from the sun, and each beam touched a village in the valley. Then I saw the world globe with all the blue oceans and I noticed how the animals that live in the seas lift their heads above the water to praise God."

As she didn't understand the English text of the song, nor did she know the Bible verses about sea creatures worshiping God, we could only thank the Holy Spirit for speaking through her. These experiences, and many others, made us realize that God has blessed her, and thereby us, with a prophetic gift.

Our daughter isn't the only reason why God sent us to Italy, but it is an important one. As we discovered, it would have been impossible to apply for adoption in the Netherlands or in France, because of our age. It is clear that it was his purpose for us to become Aisha's parents, and we feel privileged and honored that God has entrusted this precious child to our care. We can only pray that we mirror his love in raising her and preparing her for her own destination.

Another motive for being in Italy is, obviously, to make Jesus known to the people. We are here, in the heart of a nation we have come to love and respect. Yes, the scenery and cultural wealth are fascinating but, above all, the Italians themselves have become very dear to us. Many are ashamed of their own country, especially of the injustice due to misgovernment, corruption, and nepotism, but God has shown us the beauty. Italians are a warm, hospitable, and generous people, for whom family life is of paramount importance. For example, in the Netherlands it is a fact that, when you reach a certain age, you go to a nursing home. Here in Italy, it is considered *bruttissimo*–very ugly–to put your parents in such a place. You let them live in your own house and care for them until they die. To continue in the context of family, Italians adore children. Seeing a child and not kissing it or at least giving it some caress, seems impossible for both women and men. We cannot walk in the streets with Aisha without people smiling at her, saying, *"ciao, bellissima!"* or stroking her on the head and calling her *stellina* (little star). Also between adults, there is no fear of physical contact. People, including men, touch, hug, and kiss one another unreservedly, without embarrassment.

In addition, in spite of having witnessed many financial injustices committed by the national and regional administrative authorities, they still take other people at their word. Many times, from gas station attendant to dentist, we've been told, "Don't you worry about the money, just pay when you drop by next time." Even now, in times of economical crisis with an unemployment rate hitting 12.5%, people remain friendly and trustful towards one another.

We do notice some despair though, especially when they discuss the future of their children. In the course of time, we have also seen more and more people becoming afraid and depressed, whether for financial or other reasons.

After we had received the message about the power of worship from our South African friends in the summer of 2008, Jan and I sang daily until the first people joined us. In April 2010, four years after we had felt led to form a local church, we saw things beginning to move. God used Ciro, the man we met in the Orvieto gallery that contained the depressing paintings. Although he didn't believe himself, he introduced us to friends of his who were open to the gospel. One of them, Orietta, is now a faithful member of our congregation, while the other is still afraid that her in-laws will criticize her for joining us and breaking the family's Catholic tradition. We baptized Orietta in September of 2010.

In the same year, we started to have weekly prayer meetings in a bar/pizzeria in Orvieto, where we have seen people come and, in spite of wonderful answers to prayer, leave again. Then, in January 2011, we welcomed two new people into our church, an older couple, and we baptized both of them in July. Another woman, Manuela, was already a Christian when she joined us in the spring of that year.

In the meantime, we kept sharing Jesus with many people around us, and our circle extended thanks to our school-age daughter. We counseled people with problems and we prayed for—and have seen—miracles in people's lives.

Then, in September 2012, we lost the older couple. They decided to stop coming because of an extremely difficult family situation. So we were back to two people, and that's where we still are. Two great women, genuinely in love with Jesus, with a faith huge enough to move every single Umbrian hill—spiritual or otherwise—and a deep desire to see other people come to Christ. It's with them that we have moved forwards in God's plan for our local church, encouraged not only by more progressive revelation about what he wants to do through all of us in the heart of Italy, but also by the ever-edifying ministry and continuous prayer support of our international NCMI family.

By the way, God has continued to speak to us about the Italian heart. Almost two years ago, we met an American missionary couple in Tuscany, and they shared with us that God had told them to visit the geographical heart of Italy and pray for this nation. At least four cities claim to have that spot within their boundaries: Narni, Monteluco, Foligno, and Rieti. The couple chose Narni, more than thirty-five miles from our home. In the woods, close to an ancient Roman aqueduct called Formina, they found a stone benchmark, where they faithfully interceded for the country.

Their story struck Jan, because he thought God had said that the heart of the Italy was close to where we live. He went on the Internet and soon found an article about the geographical center of Italy being close to Orvieto, about six miles—as the crow flies—from our house. The authority was, would you believe, the Dutch land registry. They had used a GPS-based method, the most precise actually available. Jan, however, is convinced that there is still a small measure of error, and that it is only a matter of time before someone will discover that the exact heart of Italy is located in our house!

But seriously, although we don't understand it completely, we think that the heart of a nation is in some way important to God. Just as God considers our own heart to be the seat of our inner conviction that feeds and leads our whole being, for better or for worse, he may see the center of a country as the symbol of where the entire nation is going. The Bible says, "Keep your heart with all vigilance, for from it flow the springs of life."

Umbria, the green heart of Italy, is an empty heart as far as God is concerned. Many and impressive are the religious monuments, but there are few real disciples of Christ who desire to see the Italian people run to him and surrender to him, to find love, peace, wholeness, and a meaningful life.

God loves the Italian people and wants to make them his family members. In spite of the widespread Roman Catholic religion, most Italians don't know God. Oh, many are acquainted with him—although what they've heard about him doesn't necessarily correspond to who he really is—but most don't know him personally. The causes are numerous: misrepresentation of his character, deception by being taught traditions of men rather than Biblical truth, disappointment in the Church as an institution so that people turn their back on God altogether, secular materialism, or just plain indifference. In addition, as we read about Italy on the website of the prayer movement Operation World:

> Occultism continues to be alarmingly widespread – there are more than 150,000 practicing soothsayers, prognosticators, and healers, in contrast to around 50,000 Catholic priests! Eastern and esoteric spirituality are increasingly popular. Italians are more liable to dabble in an occult, New Age or pagan practice than

to read the Bible. Those who do pray will often pray to Padre Pio (37%) or Saint Anthony (21%) rather than to Jesus (less than 10%). Cults are active; Jehovah's Witnesses number more in Italy than all its Protestants combined.

Our mission is to plant a lampstand in this spiritual darkness. God has sent us here to make him known for who he really is, among the Italians, and in the midst of hard times. Whether it is by forming, with him, one or more local churches and/or by a revival within the Roman Catholic Church, many Italians will enter his Kingdom.

Here in Umbria, God has given me a new beginning as his daughter. He also gave Jan and me a new beginning as a couple and he gave us a new beginning as a family with Aisha. He guided every single step to that moment, and every step since, for a purpose.

Now we believe that a new beginning for his church is at hand. Only recently, God has given us the vision of a new season with fields that are white for harvest all over this region. "Look, I tell you, lift up your eyes, and see that the fields are white for harvest." God's heart aches for the Italian people, as Jesus expressed in Matthew's Gospel.

> When he saw the crowds, he had compassion for them, because they were harassed and helpless, like sheep without a shepherd. Then he said to his disciples, "The

harvest is plentiful, but the laborers are few; therefore pray earnestly to the Lord of the harvest to send out laborers into his harvest."

In spite of the seemingly impossible situation, we have faith and trust in him for a supernatural harvest, because it is *his* desire to reap! We won't give up sowing his love and truth, because the Italians need to see the way out of the darkness. They need to meet Jesus. Not the helpless baby in the manger or the dead man on the cross, but the real, living, and loving King Jesus, who calls them into his Kingdom of light. The King who ransoms people's souls and transforms their lives. We want to be shining signposts, guiding every single person we talk to closer to Christ. We *will* see his light touch every city, right here in the heart of Italy–our destination.

Afterword
By Jan

*W*hen Milly told me that the first draft of her book was ready for me to read, I was thrilled. Curious, I had sometimes tried to get a glimpse of its content, standing behind her while she worked at her laptop. In these occasions, she had always asked me friendly to wait. "You'll be the first to read it, when it's ready."

Not sure what to expect, I began reading it. Yes, I knew the story, which is partly our common story, but now got to know it from Milly's viewpoint. While going through the pages, I was touched and at times overwhelmed, with tears in my eyes. To read it all consecutively was an emotional experience.

Milly and I both have our own history. Before meeting each other, we have lived our beautiful moments and our hardships. I am the very proud father of two great sons. Unfortunately, I got divorced. Milly too has been married before. God redeemed our pasts and granted her and me a new start together, this time in him. It is only by his grace that the plans he had for us since our mothers' wombs haven't died, but come to life.

In this book, Milly describes her walk to faith. She also writes about how we, as a couple, are guided towards our purpose. The vision God gave us for our destiny is best described as the flower bud at a plant that has its roots in our youth. The bud now unfolds itself, getting clearer in both form and colors. Gradually, we are discovering the reason of our existence in such a time as this.

Going from the Netherlands to France before reaching our destination in Italy wasn't a deviation from God's plan; he intended it as an intermediary period to prepare us for the next. It was there, far away from the business world we had both worked in, that he began to work in us. On our French campsite, we learned to serve instead of being served, cooking four-course meals, waiting on people, cleaning the sanitary facilities, and always listening to our guests, who shared their lives and their problems with us. The living God transformed first me, and thus changed me into a witness towards Milly.

One thing Milly couldn't write, but I can, is that I have prayed intensely for her conversion. I have seen Milly's struggle to find Jesus from the outside, because she never allowed me to get to the inside of her fight for faith. It was not until after she became a Christian that she shared some of her feelings with me. For me, as her husband, seeing her surrender to Jesus was as if I was marrying her again, this time in Christ. She became part of his household. Suddenly, we were able to talk and share without barriers. We could start Bible school studies, prepare exams, and anxiously await the results together. The fact she always got one grade higher than I did was a joy.

As becomes clear in this book, we have not been formed within a church. We haven't taken on any church habit or influence of tradition. What we have done though is submitting to an apostolic team, because we learned that it is biblical to do so. Still, we don't follow a man-made blue print about how to "do church." We have only God's Word, which tells us, "to proclaim the gospel of the Kingdom," not to build a church. Jesus himself builds the church, based on the revelation that he is the anointed King of that Kingdom.

This book is not just about a loving, patient God, who calls people out of a lost world and redeems them for eternity, but also about how he prepares these people, almost in secret, to serve in his end time army. We wouldn't be surprised if, in these last days, the church will have to change and walk differently from how it has done for ages. We are ready for a mighty move of the Holy Spirit, in which we will leave the stage to him as the leading actor, trusting that he will guide us then, just as he has always done.

The fire for Italy that came into our hearts was impossible to explain to anybody, but we know that God has guided our steps. From the move into a house in the geographical heart of the nation to the vision for our ministry in Italy, from the amazing answers to prayers, with signs and wonders, to the completion of our family with our marvelous daughter, who is the crowning glory of our marriage; it has all been in his hand.

Lord, we give you, and only you, the credit for the content of this book. You are truly an amazing God, and it is an honor for us to serve you as a family, to work together with you, while we carry out your plans for our lives and for this great nation, Italy.

I love you, Milly, with all my heart, and I thank you for writing about our journey towards our destination.

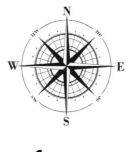

Sources

"Employment and unemployment." Posted October 31, 2013. *Italian National Institute of Statistics*. *http://www.istat.it*. Accessed November 8, 2013.

"Italy." *Operation World*. *http://www.operationworld.org*. Accessed November 7, 2013.

Jones Tobias. *The dark heart of Italy*. London, UK: Faber and Faber, 2003.

Keb'Mo. *Hand It Over*. Sony/Okeh, 1996.

LaHaye Tim F. *Jesus: Who Is He?* Colorado Springs, USA: Multnomah Books, 1997.

"L'autorità olandese Kadaster individua a Orvieto l'esatto centro geografico dell'Italia." Posted September 29, 2009. *Orvieto News*. *http://www.orvietonews.it*. Accessed November 7, 2013.

Lewis C.S. *Mere Christianity*. New York, USA: HarperCollins Publishers, 1952.

NCMI. *http://www.ncmi.net*. Accessed January 24, 2014.

Ochs Michael, Mullen David, Mullen Nicole C. *On My Knees*. Word Music, 1996.

Redman Matt. *The Heart of Worship*. EMI Christian Music Group, 1999.

Riddle Jeremy. *More Than a Friend*. Mercy/Vineyard Publishing, 2002.

Rizzo Justin. *Glory Will Cover The Earth*. Forerunner Music, 2006.

Sandidge Jerry. *Challenge to Encounter*. Springfield, USA: ICI University, 1994.

Sibthorpe Joyce. *Can you hear God?* West Sussex, England: New Wine Press, 1995.

Tenney Tommy. *The God Chasers*. Shippensburg, USA: Destiny Image, 1998.

The Big Lebowsky. Coen Joel, Coen Ethan. Gramercy. 1998. Film.

Tomlin Chris. *Shout to the Lord*. Sparrow Records, 1998.

Yong-Gi Cho David, Yong-Gi Cho Paul, Yong-Gi Paul. *Solving Life's Problems*. South Plainfield, USA: Bridge Publishing, 1980.

About the Author

*M*illy Born has a master's degree in psychology. She started her working life with an international IT company, holding jobs in technical writing and communications. In 1998, she and her husband, Jan, gave up their business careers and moved to the south of France to build and run a campsite. Five years later, they felt strongly drawn to Italy; in 2004, their life path took yet another turn when they moved to Umbria. There, amid forested hills and historic cities, Milly found not only her geographical destination, but also, after an intense struggle, her spiritual destination. Milly and Jan now pastor a Christian community. Milly loves to spend time with Jan and their daughter and, other than writing, enjoys taking long walks through the woods with their three dogs. Her favorite season in Umbria is autumn, when the heat of the Italian summer gives way to more invigorating temperatures, wisps of fog rise from the valleys in the morning, and golden sunlight intensifies the vibrant fall colors of the forests.

If you like to read more from this author, please visit her blog at http://destinationitaly.wordpress.com.